Douglas Hall's
CATS

Text by
Jonathan Hall

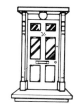

Brian Trodd Publishing House

ABYSSINIAN

Although introduced to Britain in 1868 from Abyssinia, this African breed is regarded as Egyptian in origin. The Abyssinian has a unique short, fine and close-lying coat. The coat hairs have double or treble ticking; two or three bands of darker colour on each hair. Thus it was originally called the Hare or Rabbit cat, in the mistaken belief that it was a cross between a cat and a rabbit. The usual colour is golden brown with ruddy orange markings, ticked with black. Other colours include copper- red, blue, silver, and lilac.

AFRICAN WILD CAT

The main ancestor of the domestic cat, the African Wild Cat is proportionately larger, standing 35cm (13¾″) at the shoulder, and is found all over Africa except in deserts. It lives on almost any terrain and leads a solitary and largely nocturnal existence, preying on a variety of small animals. The coat varies from light sandy through yellowish-grey to grey-brown, with either pale grey or reddish-brown/black markings—slightly tabby on the face, stripes on the flanks, and rings on the forelegs, upper hindlegs, and the end of the long, thin tail.

AMERICAN SHORTHAIR

A robust natural breed, the American Shorthair came over with the original English settlers as companions-cum-ship's cats. Although still similar to the British Shorthair, the American breed became larger and developed a less rounded head, an oval face, a longer nose, and a squarer muzzle with a firm chin on a longer neck. Large to medium in size, American Shorthairs prefer country life and being able to roam freely over large areas. The thick, even coat, not as plush as the British Shorthair, can be any colour.

AMERICAN WIREHAIR

First recorded in 1966 at Verona, New York, the American Wirehair is a natural mutation of an American Shorthair. The unique coat (of any colour) is springy to the touch and like lambswool in texture. This is because the top coat hairs are crimped and wavy along the length, hooked at the end, and thinner than normal. The fur is of medium length and tightly curled, even forming ringlets instead of waves on the head. The Wirehair has more rounded ears than the Shorthair, and has untidy whiskers.

ANGORA

The first long-haired cats in Europe and originally only white, Angoras gradually became less popular as Persian cats came to be preferred. The name comes from Ankara in Turkey, and as Angoras were introduced to Britain from France in the 16th century, they were known for a time as French cats. The Angora has quite long legs and medium-length, slightly wavy, silky hair. It has a long neck and a gently pointed face with a long straight nose, and when on the move, carries its tail horizontally over the back.

BI-COLOURED SHORTHAIR

Although pedigree records only go back about 100 years, shorthairs have existed for centuries and Bi-coloureds are no exception. Despite being exhibited at the first cat shows at the end of the 19th century, Bi-coloured cats were only recently recognised, and only then because they were found to be indispensable in breeding the elusive Tortoiseshell-and-Whites. The standard is strict; only black, blue, red, and cream with white, no white hairs in the colour, symmetrical markings evenly distributed, and not more than half white.

BLACK LONGHAIR

Known in Europe since the 16th century, and first shown in Britain in 1871, Black Longhairs or Persians were originally more akin to Angoras, with long noses and larger ears, but with subsequent breeding the snub nose and small ears are now typical. Characteristic too is a low body with short legs, a short, full tail, and the distinctive ruff or frill of long silky hair which is brushed up to form a frame for the wide, round head. Jet black is required, with no tabby, rustiness, or white hairs.

BLACK SHORTHAIR

Both Longhair and Shorthair Blacks are considered lucky in Britain nowadays, although superstitions connected with black magic, dating back to the witchhunts of the Middle Ages, still linger, especially in the rest of Europe. The Shorthair is medium to large, sturdy with short legs, deep chest and wide shoulders and rump. Short necked with rounded head, face, cheeks, and small ears, it has a short broad nose. The coat is short, dense and plush, and like the Longhair, a glossy, even jet black without rustiness or white hairs.

BLUE LONGHAIR

The beautiful Blue Persian is one of the most popular of domestic breeds. Known in Renaissance Italy and later favoured by Queen Victoria in England, they have been bred in France and England for centuries. The pale grey-blue colour comes from the dilution of black, probably with white, and by 1889 Blues had their own class at shows. Today they have a British show entirely to themselves. The Persian coat is long, at up to 15cm (6″), thick, fine, and silky, and ideally hairs are separate and stand away from the body.

BLUE POINT BALINESE

Recognised in 1963, and combining the graceful beauty and general colouring of the Siamese with a quieter voice and temperament, the Balinese is an American long-haired Siamese, named after the lithe grace of Balinese dancers. It has a long, wedge-shaped head with a straight nose, large pointed ears, a long plumed tail, and a silky, flat, ruff-less coat of 5cm (2″) plus. The points (mask, ears, legs, feet, and tail) are clearly defined solid colour, generally either chocolate, blue, lilac, red, cream, tortoiseshell or tabby.

BLUE TABBY LONGHAIR

'Tabby' comes from tabbisilk, the English word for watered silk from the Attabiya district of Baghdad, striped similar to the cat's markings. The first domesticated cats were tabbies, as most wild cats were striped, and Tabby Persians were recorded in Europe in the 16th century. Most Tabby markings are black, but the Blue has deep slate blue markings. Long hair distorts the Tabby standard, which includes the 'M' mark on the forehead, butterfly shoulder markings, three parallel lines along the spine, and unbroken rings on the legs, tail, neck, and upper chest.

BOBCAT

Also known as the Bay Lynx, the Bobcat is smaller than the Canada Lynx, with thinner legs, smaller feet, and less tufted ears (if at all). It stands 45-58cm (17¾-22¾″) at the shoulder, and the short coat is any shade of buff/brown, spotted and lined with black and brownish black, and the backs of the ears and the upper tip of the short tail are black. It lives throughout North America in virtually any terrain, and is mainly nocturnal. Bobcats mainly eat small mammals, especially rabbits, hares, and ground- squirrels.

BOMBAY

Not Indian, but a Brown Burmese-Black American Shorthair cross, the Bombay combines the black colour and robustness of the American Shorthair and the sleek glossy coat and even-tempered affection of the Burmese. The coat and colour are important; the coat is very short and satiny and the colour is black to the roots with no white hair or patches. It has large copper eyes, a broad nose, and medium-sized ears rounded at the tips. It thrives on activity and human companionship.

BRITISH BLUE

After a great decline during the Second World War, but enjoying re- establishment since the 1950s, the Blue is one of the most popular of all British Shorthairs, being quiet and of even temperament. The Shorthair coat is resilient, dense and plush and the Blue's coat is a light to medium blue from root to tip, with no shading, white hairs, or tabby markings. Shorthairs have large round eyes with the width of an eye between them,and are copper, orange, or gold in colour. The smallish ears are rounded at the tips, and set well apart.

BROWN TABBY LONGHAIR

Relatively few are seen at shows because of the difficulty in obtaining the correct standard of colouring. The long, flowing coat is a rich tawny sable to coppery-brown, with no white hairs and jet black markings—delicate, unbroken, and pencil-thin down the face and curving on the cheeks with deep symmetrical bands on the flanks. Any blotches have to be on both sides and circled by unbroken rings, with a double row of 'buttons' from chest to stomach, particularly difficult due to the long frill between the front legs.

BROWN BURMESE

While similar cats can be traced back to 15th century Thailand, the present-day breed arose out of a brown female of Oriental type, imported to America from Burma in 1930, which was mated with a Siamese. First appearing in Britain in 1948, the Burmese is medium-sized, with long, slender legs, and is heavier than it appears. The glossy coat has a close satin texture. Brown, an even, dark chocolate, was the first colour to be bred and recognised. Other subsequent colours include blue, champagne, lilac, red, and cream.

CHARTREUSE

Said to have been brought from South Africa by Carthusian monks, famous in Grenoble for their greenish-yellow liqueur, the Chartreuse is virtually identical to the British Blue Shorthair. Originally larger than the Blue, the Chartreuse has a greyer blue coat, a less rounded head, and a deeper chest, but recent breeding has brought the two so close together that the same standard is generally accepted for both. The French authoress, Colette, a life-long lover of Persians, had a Chartreuse as her companion when she died in 1954.

CHINCHILLA LONGHAIR

In Britain the Chinchilla differs from other longhairs in being daintier and more delicate with finer bones, whereas American Chinchillas are larger and closer to other Persians. Although fragile, they have a hardy nature. 'Chinchilla' is a misnomer—the South American animal of this name has grey fur, while the Chinchilla cat's coat is pure white tipped with black, giving a shimmering silver appearance. Developed in 1902 from a Silver Tabby -Blue Tabby cross, and immediately popular, they enjoyed the patronage of Princess Victoria, Queen Victoria's grand-daughter.

CHEETAH

The most streamlined of cats, and uniquely unable to retract its claws, the Cheetah can reach 100Km/h 65 mph and preys mainly on gazelles, antelopes and wildebeest calves. It is the same length as the Leopard but taller, standing at 76-83 cm (30-31¾″) and slimmer with a rounder, smaller head and a tail of more than half the body length. The coarse coat varies between yellowish grey and tawny fawn, paler underneath, with round black spots. Today the Cheetah is scarce except in African National Parks, its preference for daylight hunting making it easy prey for poachers.

CORNISH REX

Rex refers to a natural mutation in the structure of the coat hairs, resulting in a wavy coat, soft, fine, dense, and without guard hairs, first discovered in 1950 in an otherwise normal litter on Bodmin Moor, Cornwall. The short, plush coat can be any colour, and it curls or ripples all over, especially on the back, flanks and tail, which is long, fine, and whip-like. They have slender bodies with long, straight legs, and medium-long heads with highly-set large ears, rounded at the tips, and oval eyes.

CREAM SHORTHAIR

Originally considered freaks when they appeared occasionally in Tortoiseshell litters, British Cream Shorthairs were recognised in 1920. They are rare both because of the difficulty in obtaining an even cream coat, neither 'hot' (too orange) nor fawn, without tabby markings, white hairs, or shadow rings on the tail and because blue is a genetic dilution of black, and cream is diluted red (or orange), which as a colour is sex-linked to produce less females than males. However, Cream females are obtained by mating a Blue-Cream female with a Cream male.

CYMRIC

Otherwise known as the
Longhaired Manx, the Cymric is
essentially American, as Manx
cats in Britain are short-coated.
The Manx possesses no tail
at all, has a round, rabbity
appearance, the short back
being arched from shoulder
to well-rounded rump, with
the hind legs longer than
the front. Although the
original shorthair Manx hail
from the Isle of Man,
longhair kittens first
appeared in Canada in the
1960s. The medium-long
double coat, of any colour,
is thick and cottony
underneath with a silky,
glossy topcoat.

DEVON REX

Like the Cornish, the Devon Rex appeared in Britain in 1950, but surprisingly, crossing them produced normal-coated kittens without exception. The Devon Rex has a coarser coat than the Cornish, due to minute guard hairs, and it is short, fine, wavy, soft, and any colour. With a long tail and large low-set ears, the mischievous Devon Rex has a shorter, elfin face with large, oval, slightly slanted eyes. Rex was first recognised as a breed in 1967, and in 1980 the first of all Rex cat shows was held in Kentucky.

EGYPTIAN MAU

Also known as the Oriental Spotted Shorthair, the Egyptian Mau is the only naturally spotted Oriental-type cat. Thought to be descended from cats revered in ancient Egypt in the form of the gods Isis and Bast, the Mau (the Egyptian word for 'cat' and 'to see') first appeared in Europe at the Rome cat show in 1950. The coat is silver, bronze, smoke, or pewter (fawn) with darker, symmetrical spots and stripes that can be seen both on the skin and as Abyssinian-like double ticking on individual hairs.

EUROPEAN WILD CAT

Larger than the domestic cat, the European or Forest Wild cat is more sturdily built, with a broader head, and a shorter, blunter tail. The dense, long coat is yellowish-grey, a darker grey on the back and yellower underneath, with dark markings which consist of about five stripes from forehead to neck merging into one dorsal line to the tail, from which emanate the stripes on the flanks. Inhabiting woodlands and treeless rocky terrain in Scotland and most of Europe, this cat preys on small rodents.

HAVANA

The Havana was the first shorthair breed with a Siamese body type, but without Siamese colouring. Instead its coat is a rich, warm, chestnut brown, called Havana because of its similarity in colour to the tobacco in a Havana cigar. The Havana is well-balanced, slender, and svelte, with a long body, neck and head, long legs, a long, whiplike tail, largish pricked (forward-pointing) ears, and vivid green eyes. The lustrous, close lying coat is very short and fine in texture, and evenly and solidly coloured.

JAGUAR

The Jaguar is the largest cat in South and Central America, where it is called 'el tigre'. Fond of tropical forests with plenty of water and swamps, it preys nocturnally on aquatic and terrestrial animals and birds, from fish and turtles to caymans, from capybaras and monkeys to wild pigs and horses. Standing 68-76 cm (26¾-30″) tall they are powerfully built, and the coat varies from yellow through reddish-yellow to rust-brown, paler underneath, with black tail-rings, spots, blotches, and rosettes enclosing spots on a darker background.

JAPANESE BOBTAIL

Native to Japan, China, and Korea, the Japanese Bobtail or Mi-Ke cat has a characteristic short bobbed tail, the thick hair of which produces a fluffy pom-pom. They often stand with one paw lifted, as if greeting or welcoming, and for centuries Japanese prints and paintings have depicted similar cats doing exactly this. Long and slender, with long hindlegs, high cheekbones, and large, oval, slanted eyes, the Bobtail has a soft, silky, medium-length coat that is any colour but usually tricolour (black, red, and white).

KORAT

Known for centuries in Thailand, this natural breed originated in Korat, an area north-east of Bangkok, where these greatly-prized cats are called Si-Sawat, or 'good fortune'. First appearing in Britain in 1972, Korats have large brilliant green eyes and a short, glossy, fine coat that is solidly silver-blue all over, tipped with silver to give a distinctive sheen. They have heart-shaped faces and highly-set large ears, and as they move with curved backs, the coat ripples or breaks along the spine.

LEOPARD

Perhaps the most athletic big cat, excelling at running, jumping, tree-climbing, and swimming, the Leopard, though 64-78 cm (25-30¾″) tall, resembles the domestic cat with its round head, short nose, and long, thin tail. The coat ranges from straw to ochre, white underneath, with black spots, blotches, tail-rings and rosettes, which are smaller than the Jaguar's. Found in Africa, Asia, and Arabia, and adaptable to any terrain, the stealthy, secretive and solitary Leopard will eat anything from lizards to large deer.

LYNX

Found in Canada, Europe, and Asia, the Lynx is a large, powerfully-built cat, 65-70 cm (25½-27½") tall, with long sturdy legs, a short tail, triangular ears with distinctive black tufts, almost mane-like side whiskers, and well-furred paws. It has a yellowish-brown coat, with spots that are dark or light according to where it lives. Although adaptable, the Lynx prefers old forests with fallen trees and dense undergrowth, and it mainly preys on hares and rabbits, as well as birds, small rodents and other mammals.

MAINE COON CAT

This shy American 'gentle giant' has a distinctive quiet, chirping voice. It developed from longhaired cats brought to Maine, New England, in the 19th century by Asian traders, which mated with local shorthairs, giving its appearance of being shorthaired in front and longhaired along the back and stomach. It was called Coon cat because of its similarity to a raccoon, with its long fur and, as a tabby, its colouring and ringed tail. Long-bodied, with a proportionately small head, the Maine Coon's silky coat is any colour.

MANX

Tail-less cats have been known for centuries in Japan, Russia, and Malaysia. Manx arrived via Eastern traders on the Isle of Man about 250 years ago and, isolated without competition, they flourished, becoming lucky mascots synonymous with the Isle itself. Nicknamed 'Rumpy' from the rounded, prominent hindquarters and long hindlegs, and 'Rabbit cat' from its gait, the Manx has a large, round head, a long nose, and wide, pointed ears, a short back, a hollow where its tail should be, and a double coat that is any colour.

NORWEGIAN FOREST CAT

The Norsk Skogkatt, or Norwegian Forest Cat, evolved from matings between European Shorthairs and Asian Longhairs brought to Scandinavia by traders. A rough, active, outdoor life in harsh climates created a hardy disposition and double coat—a tight, woolly undercoat and a smooth, oily, waterproof topcoat of any colour. Domesticated but freedom-loving, the long-bodied, muscular Forest cat has long legs with wide feet, a long neck that has a ruff in winter, and a triangular head with a long, straight nose and large pointed ears.

OCELOT

The nocturnal Ocelot lives in South and Central American forests, and is 40-50 cm (15¾-19¾″) tall. Known as the Painted Leopard because of its decorative coat: tawny golden yellow on the head and down the back and silvery on the flanks, with rows of dark spots and chainlike streaks and blotches that form long, rectangular spots of a darker colour bordered in black. It preys on birds, snakes, small mammals, and the young of larger mammals, while hunters slaughter Ocelots so that their beautiful coats can adorn humans.

ODD-EYED WHITE SHORTHAIR

There are four types of White Shorthair: Blue-eyed, Orange-eyed, Green-eyed (non-pedigree), and Odd-eyed. Pure white cats are not very common because Blue-eyed Whites tend to be deaf. Those with orange, gold, or copper eyes are not, but Odd-eyed cats are often deaf on the blue side, although even a few darker hairs in the coat signifies the ability to hear. Deaf cats are disadvantaged because, for example, they cannot hear approaching traffic and a mother cannot hear her kittens.

PEKE-FACED LONGHAIR

Bred in America since the 1930s, Peke-faced Persians occur in the litters of Red and Red Tabby Persians. Sometimes cream-coloured, they resemble Persians in every respect except the face, which looks like a Pekinese dog, with a very short indented nose, a domed forehead, and large jowls. Because of its snub nose, this breed of cat can suffer from blocked tear ducts, and breathing difficulties if its jaws are not in alignment. However, Peke-faced Persians are friendly, intelligent, quiet, and companionable.

PUMA

Found in North America and in parts of South America, the Puma, Cougar, or Mountain Lion stands 60-76 cm (23½-30″) tall and varies in uniform coloration from shades of red to shades of grey. It has a long, lithe body and a small head with a short, rounded face, small, short, rounded ears, and a long neck. The rump is higher than the shoulders because the muscular hindlegs are longer than the forelegs. Nocturnal, adaptable, and a wide-ranging wanderer, the Puma mainly eats deer and smaller mammals.

RED TABBY SHORTHAIR

Shorthaired Tabbies can be Brown, Red, Silver, Blue, or Cream, and each of these can be in slightly different coat patterns, namely Classic, Spotted, and Mackerel, the latter distiguished by an unbroken line from head to tail, with as many as possible thin stripes coming from it down the flanks. The most common and popular pattern is the Classic, with Silver being the favourite colour. Red Tabbies, mistakenly associated with marmalade or ginger alley cats, are actually a deep, rich red with darker red markings.

RUSSIAN BLUE

First shown in Britain at the end of the 19th century and said to originate in Archangel, Russia, Russian Blues have also been called Blue Foreign, Archangel, Maltese, and Spanish cats. Quiet, affectionate, and slender, Russian Blues have a medium dark blue double coat, which is short, thick, very fine, and tipped with silver to give a sheen. Although of Oriental type, the head is shorter than a Siamese, with a straight nose and large, vertically-set pointed ears, so thin-skinned as to be almost transparent.

SEAL-POINT BIRMAN

Introduced to Britain in 1965, the Birman, the Sacred Cat of Burma, was originally kept in Burmese temples centuries ago. According to legend, Birmans were white but, with the death of the high priest, when invaders threatened Burma, his cat miraculously changed to gold, with dark earth-brown feet, tail, face and ears, and blue, not yellow eyes. The paws stayed white, having touched the priest's head. The long-bodied Seal-point Birman has a long golden beige coat with dark brown mask, ears, legs, and tail.

SEAL-POINT SIAMESE
First shown in Britain in 1885 but known for two centuries before that as the Royal Cats of Siam (Thailand), Siamese are among the most popular of breeds. Highly intelligent, mysterious and extrovert, a Siamese has a long neck and head, a whiplike tail, long legs, a straight nose, blue eyes, and large, pointed ears. They dislike being alone or ignored, are prone to illness, and can be very noisy. The fine, glossy, close-lying coat of the Seal-point is warm cream/fawn with dark brown points.

SCOTTISH FOLD

The distinctive feature of this gentle
cat is the way its ears fold forwards
and downwards. Otherwise
resembling an ordinary shorthair, the
first British example of a Scottish Fold
occurred in a litter of Scottish farm
cats in 1961. Known in 18th century
China, the mutant gene responsible
for the alteration of the ear is not
associated with colour, so Scottish
Folds have coats of many hues. It is
not painful or problematic for the cat
to have the upper half of its ear
covering the opening.

SMOKE PERSIAN

Like the Chinchilla Longhair, the
Smoke Longhair has a white coat with
contrasting tips to the hairs, but
whereas the hairs of the Chinchilla
are tipped on an eighth of the total
length, the Smoke Persian's coat hairs
are heavily coloured on at least half
the hair length, so that the white only
shows when they move. Known in
Britain since 1865, Smoke Persians
can be Black, Blue, Red, Tortoiseshell,
or Cream. However, strong sunlight
can bleach the colour out, and the
coat reacts to dampness too.

SNOW LEOPARD

The long-bodied Snow Leopard or Ounce has long, woolly fur that is smoke-grey with a yellowish tinge on the flanks, whiter underneath, with black spots on the head, large blurred rosettes around smaller spots on the body, and rings on the well-furred tail. Inhabiting high, inaccessible, mountainous regions, especially the Himalayas, Hindu Kush, and Tibet, the powerful, agile Ounce stands about 60 cm (23½″) tall and eats wild sheep and goats, deer, birds, and marmots. Poachers have made it suffer greatly for its beautiful fur.

SOMALI

Affectionate and extremely quiet, the Somali is a long-haired Abyssinian. They first appeared in Abyssinian litters during the 1960s, the long hair probably due to mating with longhairs. They have large ears, well-tufted inside, and large almond-shaped eyes with 'spectacles' of light fur around them. The coat is medium-long, full, dense, and silky, long on the neck and hindlegs, and either golden brown with black markings and ticking on ear-tips and end of tail, or Sorrel (red) with chocolate markings.

SPHYNX

The Moon Cat or Sphynx is particularly unusual as it is hairless. Hairless kittens occasionally appear in litters, but the Sphynx was developed as a breed in Canada from 1966 onwards, thus obtaining the name Canadian Hairless. Long, fine-boned, and muscular, the Sphynx is hot to the touch and does not feel the cold. However, seating leaves a residue that has to be regularly sponged off. The ears are large, there is a short covering of velvety hair on the points, and the skin is any colour.

SPOTTED TABBY

The favourite 'Spottie' colours are Silver, then Brown, both with black spots, and then Red, which has deep red markings. It has the characteristic tabby 'M' mark on the forehead, and an unbroken line from the outer corner of the eyes to the back of the head. The tabby stripes are broken up into numerous, well-defined, oval, round, or rosette spots, including the line along the spine, a double row of 'buttons' on the chest or stomach, and spots or broken rings on the tail and legs.

TABBY

Tabby coats are very common among pet cats, and many domestic shorthairs are varieties of Brown Tabby. A comparison with the coat of the European and African Wild Cat shows that the spotted or striped cats, as depicted in Ancient Egyptian manuscripts and wall-paintings, were the first to be domesticated. The Brown Tabby shorthair has a broad, round head, small ears, and large round eyes, with dense black markings on top of a brilliant sable, coppery-brown ground colour.

TEMMINCK'S CAT

Closely related to the African Golden Cat, Temminck's Cat (or Asiatic Golden Cat) has a dense, harsh coat which varies from golden brown to golden red and dark brown, and is unlikely to have spots. On the cheeks and from the inner corners of the eyes upwards are white streaks bordered with black. It stands 50-55 cm (19½-21½″) tall, and inhabits densely-wooded rocky areas in Northern India, Nepal, China, Tibet, Malaysia, and Thailand, preying on birds and mammals up to the size of small deer and water buffalo calves.

TIGER

Over three metres (118″) long and over one metre (39½″) at the shoulder, the Tiger is found in Nepal, India, Thailand, Malaysia, China, Tibet, Siberia, and Mongolia, adapting to the environment and inhabiting any sort of forest or riverside vegetation. The Siberian Tiger's coat is longer-haired, paler, and less striped than the Bengal Tiger, which is reddish orange/brown, white underneath, with asymmetrical grey, brown, or black stripes that are individually and infinitely varied. Water-loving and mainly nocturnal, the silent, solitary Tiger eats mainly deer and wild pigs.

TONKINESE

Developed in North America during the 1960s, the Tonkinese is a Siamese-Burmese cross. Active, friendly, and affectionate, the highly curious 'Tonk' is likely to get lost, so many owners give it the run of a large, fenced-in enclosure and take it for walks on a lead. The lithe, well-muscled Tonkinese has long legs and medium, pricked, rounded ears. The neck is long—but shorter than the Siamese—and the soft, close-lying coat is brown, beige, blue, or silver, lighter underneath, with darker points.

TORTOISESHELL AND WHITE LONGHAIR

Called the Chintz Cat because of the bright, bold patches of black, red, and cream on white, and called the Calico in America, this striking cat is a female-only variety. Mating bi-coloured males with Tortie-and-White will have a stunning assortment of colours. The shades of the three colours vary, and can produce a coat with blue (diluted black) patches as well, called Dilute Calico or Blue Tortoiseshell-and-White.

TORTOISESHELL BURMESE

The first Blue Burmese kitten, Sealcoat Seal Surprise, was born in 1955 and other colours soon followed: Red, Cream, Chocolate, and Lilac. When Red or Cream Burmese are mated with Brown, Blue, Chocolate, or Lilac Burmese, they produce Tortoiseshell kittens. While Brown and Blue Torties were bred in 1964, the more elusive Chocolate and Lilac Torties were only registered in 1973. The Brown (Normal) and Chocolate Tortie's coats mix with shades of Red (orange), whereas the Blue and Lilac Torties mix colours with shades of Cream.

TORTOISESHELL SHORTHAIR

The Tortoiseshell coat is a mixture of black and dark and light areas of orange, evenly intermingled and covering the whole body. Tortoiseshell cats have existed for centuries, and were exhibited at the first cat shows. Healthy, gentle, attractive, and playful, they are uncommon and difficult to breed, as any Tortoiseshell males are born sterile, making it a female-only variety. A 'Tortie' female mating with a Black, Red, or Cream male can produce Tortie kittens, but there is no guarantee that even one Tortoiseshell kitten will result.

TURKISH VAN

Introduced to Britain in 1956, this breed originates from the isolated area of Lake Van in Turkey, and is distinguished by chalk-white fur with an auburn-orange tail, ringed in a darker shade, and unique auburn-orange markings on the face, either side of the forehead above the round, light amber eyes. Even kittens have these facial markings. Strong, hardy, silky, straight fur grows long during the winter and moults in spring and summer.

SURREY IN 1815

The Landscape Histories

Editor: Peter Lavery

Warwickshire in 1790
The West Riding of Yorkshire in 1842
Sussex in 1839
Surrey in 1815
Lancashire in 1648
Essex in 1603
Norfolk and Suffolk in 1733
Buckinghamshire and Bedfordshire in 1720

A. H. Lock

Surrey in 1815

OSPREY

Contents

Published in 1974 by
Osprey Publishing Ltd, P.O. Box 25
707 Oxford Road, Reading, Berkshire

ISBN 0 85045 179 5

The illustrations numbered 8, 9, 14, 15 and 43
are reproduced by courtesy of The National
Portrait Gallery, London; 10, 38 and 42
by courtesy of The National Trust; and 2 by
courtesy of Radio Times Hulton Picture
Library.

Filmset and printed by BAS Printers Limited,
Wallop, Hampshire

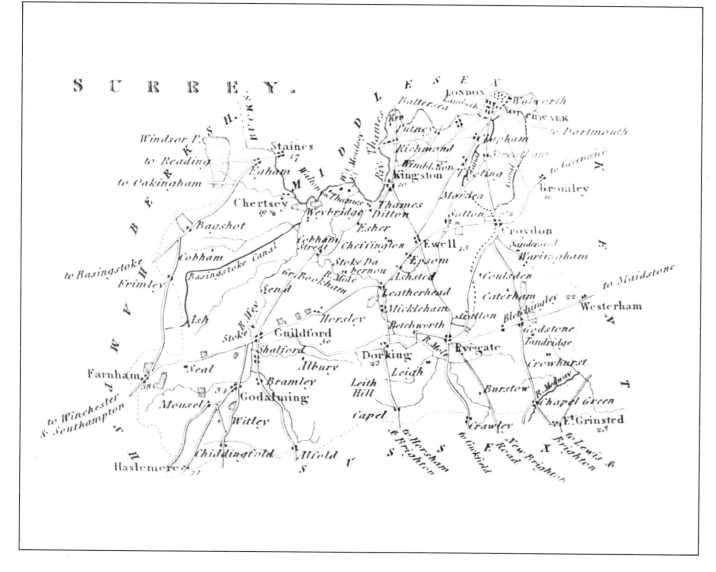

1. Map of Surrey, showing the 1815 boundaries. A population of about 350,000 lived in an area of 759 square miles.

1. Landscape and communications

In 1815 the county of Surrey was somewhat larger than it is today, extending over most of what is now south-west London south of the Thames. Besides the populous boroughs of Southwark (with over 70,000 residents) and Lambeth (over 40,000) in the most densely inhabited corner of Surrey, the county included many villages and hamlets which are today London's suburbs, such as Brixton, Blackheath, Dulwich, Camberwell, Battersea, Clapham, Wandsworth and Streatham.

With a vastly smaller population in 1815, Surrey was said 'to present, perhaps, as large a portion of beauty and deformity as any county in the kingdom'. To quote a contemporary description:

Here vast naked heaths impart an air of wildness, which is strongly contrasted with the numberless beauties strewed by the hand of art over its surface. . . . In a county where the soils and elevations are so various, the climate also must of course vary considerably. It is the general opinion that less rain falls in most parts of Surrey than in the metropolis, or in the vale of London, so that the climate may, upon the whole, be regarded as dry. . . . But the southern border must necessarily be moist and damp, from the nature of the soil, the flatness of the surface, and the immense number of trees which cover it and obstruct ventilation. . . . The spring is in general early, and here vegetation is not so often checked by frosty mornings, and cold, raw, easterly winds, as in some of the more southern counties. The summers are commonly dry and warm; and the harvest early, generally commencing in the first ten days of August.

Most of the county's northern boundary was formed by the Thames, the great river which had helped make London the largest port in the world. From the capital city goods were shipped inland by horse-drawn and sailing barges; by 1815 the river was linked to the central canal system and thus to many distant parts of Britain.

From earliest times the Thames held an abundant supply of fish, and salmon and trout could be caught easily. The river was also thick with eels; they would swim up the Thames in such numbers that they could be caught with sieves and buckets. But gradual pollution of the river started in the early nineteenth century and was driving these tasty fish away. However, in the west of the county, near Chobham and Frensham, and in the south-east, near Godstone, were several ponds 'employed for the purpose of feeding fish for the London market'. Water-mills were then as much a part of the English scene as the rivers and streams on which they stood. Along the rivers Wey, Tillingbourne, Wandle, Mole, Blackwater, Hogsmill and the Bournebrook, over 120 water-mills were at work busily producing fine flour, hog-pollard, horse-pollard*, or coarse bran. Millstones had to be constantly dressed, and flying stone-dust, splinters, and fragments of steel from dressing-bits caused a facial disfigurement which was known as 'the miller's coat-of-arms'.

*pollard – fine flour.

2. The Frost Fair on the Thames. Thousands flocked to this scene of sports and pastimes.

3. Richmond. 'At this place there is a bridge of five stone arches over the Thames, which is here about 300 feet wide. It was finished in 1777, at an expense of £26,000.'

on an icy stretch extending from Blackfriars Bridge to London Bridge, which was named 'City Road'. Swings, book-stalls, dancing in a barge, suttling-booths, skittle alleys, and almost every feature of a fair on land appeared now on the Thames. 'The ice seemed to be a solid rock and presented a truly picturesque appearance . . . in many parts mountains of ice up-heaved resembled the rude interior of a stone quarry.' Each day brought a fresh crowd of pedlars to sell their wares, and the greatest rubbish of all sorts was racked up and sold at double and treble the cost. The water-men profited exceedingly!

Communications in England advanced immeasur-ably in the previous century, when many of the country's canals were built, allowing vital goods to be carried as easily and cheaply as by sea. The Wey Navigation extended from Weybridge to Guildford and Godalming, 'whence timber, plank, hoops, bark, flour, paper and wrought iron of various sorts, are sent in considerable quantities to London'. A second canal, from Basingstoke to the Thames, entered Surrey near Dradbrook and joined the Wey near Westby: 'the principal article conveyed upon it is timber'.

The proposed Surrey Canal was begun with 'a dock at Rotherhithe, capable of containing about 100 sail of square-rigged vessels'. Only part of the actual canal was built. By 1814 the dock was prospering so well by itself that the rest of the project was abandoned. The Croydon Canal to Rotherhithe, completed in 1809, passed mostly through Kent.

At the same time the character of road travel was changing. The genius of Telford and Macadam was

Of the river Wandle it was said: 'in its course of rather more than ten miles, it turns near forty mills of different kinds, and is said to furnish employment for about 2,000 people'. Another stream, the Hogsmill, was notable 'for supplying several gun-powder mills at Ewell and Malden, and a large corn-mill at Kings-ton'.

Long, intensely cold periods had recently been common. In the winter of the previous year the Thames had frozen over, and a complete Frost Fair was held

4. The Obelisk (left) in St George's Fields was a major road junction south of the Thames. A carriage is stopping at the toll gate (centre). The large building to the left of it is the Surrey Theatre, opened in 1782.

beginning to provide the country with smooth-metalled highways. Previously, even on main roads, huge pools of water and ruts deep enough to break a horse's leg had been commonplace, and it was then freely admitted: 'The turnpike roads of this county in general are not distinguished for excellence, or judicious management.' (A turnpike road was financed by the setting up of toll-gates which obliged the road's

users to contribute to its maintenance, rather than leave this entirely as a burden on the local parish.)

This year saw a proposal for the formation of a new carriage road, to be called the New-Surrey and Kent Road (now the famous Old Kent Road):

From the High Kent Road, near New Cross, a beautiful commodious Road branches out, leading thro' Peckham to Camberwell; and it is now proposed to continue that line in

5. Heavily loaded waggons were a familiar sight, toiling up and down the Surrey roads.

a straight direction from Union Row, Camberwell to pass thro' the centre of Bowyer Lane, Lorrimore Fields, and to communicate with the Surrey Road, Kennington. From thence the present Roads lead into the interior of Surrey, and through Vauxhall communicating with the Great Western Road, by way of Battersea Bridge. The erection of the intended new Bridge of Vauxhall will render this road still more desirable and it will likewise open a more direct communication from the West End of the Town to the delightful rural villages of Dulwich, Norwood and parts adjacent.

Bridges were also the key to better communications. A plan to put another bridge across the Thames attracted immediate response. The first stone of

Southwark bridge was laid by Lord Keith in the centre of the river on 23 May 1815. Its original name was Trafalgar Bridge.

Stage-coaches were now operating along most of the usable roads of the country. These public-service coaches, with their melodious horns blown by red-coated guards, ran so punctually that men set their watches by them. The better-known Surrey stage-coaches running in 1815 were:

The Union: London – Kingston – Esher – Guildford (journey time 4 hours).

The Times: London – Morden – Epsom – Leatherhead – Guildford (journey time 4 hours).

The Star: London – Morden – Epsom – Leatherhead – Dorking – Horsham (journey time 4½ hours).

The Red Rover: London – Kingston – Esher – Guildford – Farnham – Alton – Winchester – Southampton (journey time 8 hours).

Fares varied. Inside seats cost between 4*d*. and 5*d*. per mile, and from 2*d*. to 3*d*. outside on a fast coach, with somewhat cheaper fares on the slower coaches. Winter travellers occupying outside seats were offered the following advice:

To attain the maximum comfort which the circumstances admit, they should drink a tankard of good ale cold from the tap, and rub their hands, ears and faces with snow immediately they start. This will produce a more lasting and agreeable glow than any other means.

A letter to the *Scourge* in 1815 complained of dangerous overloading of stage-coaches:

On Sunday evening between the hours of 6 and 7 p.m. the Guildford coach passed through the turnpike at the Obelisk with 14 passengers on the roof of the coach! Five in the basket and two with the coachman on the box, making, with six inside passengers and one child in the whole twenty-eight passengers! When laws are made against such practices they should be put into execution.

Some horrible accidents occurred. When the Worthing Cross Coach was passing through Mickleham, Surrey, one day in July,

. . . one of the horses became restive, and got his head under the pole; a lady, on the outside, seeing that the coach must be overturned, jumped from the roof, and at the instant, the coach fell with a dreadful crash upon her, and she survived but a few minutes.

Incidents of highway robbery were still occasionally reported. On the evening of Monday 11 December,

. . . two persons, apparently Naval Officers, took a coach off the stand at Stone's End, and ordered the coachman to drive to Clapham, and go round by South Lambeth; when a little way beyond Lark-hall-lane they stopped the coach, and jumping out, one of them held a pistol to the coachman's head, while the other rifled his pockets of upwards of £2.

The country's first iron railway, using horse-traction, was opened in 1803 between Wandsworth and Croydon. Horses pulled trains of waggons mounted on the rails. Soon the line was extended to Merstham, whence it carried stone and lime from the quarries. A large basin, capable of holding thirty barges, was constructed at Wandsworth, and this junction acted as a transfer area for goods between the Thames and the horse-drawn waggons. People expressed surprise at the great weights the horses could pull. At a demonstration at Merstham twelve waggons each carrying three tons were pulled six miles by one horse, with apparently no great effort, in 1 hour 41 minutes. The owner, who had won a wager by this feat, then attached another four waggons and ordered fifty of his workmen to climb on. Incredible though it seems, a magnificent shire-horse then moved the waggon-train without apparent distress. The total load was over fifty-five tons! All the same, this railway never really proved a commercial success. Despite such new methods of communication, goods were still being carried by pack horses over rural parts of Surrey.

2. Politics and the military

Dawn on 18 June 1815 started singularly cold. A depressing half-light revealed the British troops, mustered two miles from the village of Waterloo, to be drenched to the skin.

These troops were mainly drawn, except for regiments like Picton's Highlanders, from the arable counties of southern England. Thus a great many men from Surrey stood in the ranks. They had enlisted in Kingston, Guildford, Farnham; they came from villages and hamlets stretching across the county – yeomen who had been forced to give up their smallholdings, men who had lost jobs and tied cottages on the farms. The hardships of poverty resulting from a prevailing economic necessity had been a cross these erstwhile farm labourers had to bear. Redistribution of unregistered fields and common lands surrounding villages, following private Acts of Parliament designed to rationalize uneconomical holdings, brought unemployment – and recruits to fight the French.

By 10 a.m. on the 18th the sun was well up; as uniforms dried out, the low morale of the troops rose. Underfoot a foul-smelling quagmire made movement difficult – nightlong thunderstorms had bucketed water out of the heavens. Later that morning Wellington, accompanied by his staff, cantered round the lines. The troops noted that they looked as cheerful and unconcerned as if they were riding to a hunt meeting in England.

As visibility improved, Napoleon's troops with their glittering helmets and cuirasses could be seen on the ridge of La Belle Alliance two kilometres away. Faint shouts of '*Vive l'Empereur*' came across the valley.

'I tell you,' Napoleon said to his chief of staff, 'Wellington is a bad general, the British are bad troops, and this will be a picnic!'

He was fatally wrong. It was not a picnic for Napoleon, nor for Blücher who supported the British, nor for Wellington and his rosy-faced yokels from the plough.

After the battle, as darkness fell, Wellington wearily turned his horse towards his headquarters and rode in silence through the bloody shambles of the battlefield. He picked his way through 15,000 dead of his own army and 30,000 dead or dying Frenchmen. At 9 o'clock he met Blücher and the two men embraced.

'*Quelle affaire!*' said Wellington; this was about all the French he knew. It was adequate.

Within a matter of weeks, after a series of triumphant marches through Paris, British troops began to filter back to their home depots. In no time many were discharged. Then they trudged back to their families – and the problem of finding work on the land.

George III sat on the throne. He was now an old man and his recurring illness meant even more frequent periodic withdrawals from public life and duties. In the very first week of 1815 it was reported: 'The King's disorder continues unabated, but His Majesty has passed the last month in a very tranquil state.'

Queen Charlotte, however, continued to be seen in public. One day in September,

The Queen, Princesses Augusta, Elizabeth and Mary, with several of the nobility, royal attendants, etc. went to Virginia Water on a fishing party; and dined in tents on the banks of that romantic lake: the band of the 5th regiment attended. The young ladies of Miss Bird's boarding-school, Egham House, passing by, were affably directed by Her Majesty to approach, treated with refreshments, kindly noticed individually, and retained some hours, during which the band played several times, and the young ladies to the number of fifteen couples, danced on the shaded lawn, to the great pleasure of the Royal Party.

During the King's incapacity, his eldest son George, the Prince Regent, with his favourites ruled the country. His latest lady-friend and adviser-in-chief was an exquisite grandmother, the Marchioness of Hertford, and with her he behaved like a lovesick schoolboy. 'Prinny', though not yet fifty-four, was enormously fat, and to many of his contemporaries he appeared a grotesque, flouncing tyrant. In 1815 it was revealed that over the last three years his new furniture for Carlton House had cost the country £260,000, and that his debts now stood at £339,000 – yet an ordinary labourer's yearly income scarcely exceeded £30!

Surrey had one royal residence, the White House, at Kew; the building of another nearby was commenced in 1801 (both were later demolished, and only the older Dutch House now remains). Sir Richard Phillips described Kew as the Bastille Palace and wondered why the King was content to look over the

6. A caricature of George, the Prince Regent, after whom the years around 1815 have been called the 'Regency' period.

7. The new palace at Kew. 'This structure, which is of the castellated form, and in its architecture an imitation of the style of the middle of the 16th century, is from the designs of James Wyatt, Esq. and as yet unfinished.'

Appointed Commander-in-Chief of the Army in 1798, his lack of success in the field was much criticized:

> My name is York,
> I draw a cork
>   Much better than I fight,
> The soldiers knew,
> As well as you
>   That what I say is right.

Worse still, in 1809 a scandal forced him to resign. A handsome adventuress called Mrs Clarke had established herself in his favour, and drifted into the habit of selling commissions and promotions on the strength of her intimacy with the Commander-in-Chief. However, the Duke was reinstated in 1811 and rendered valuable service to his country.

Lambeth Palace was, of course, the residence of the Archbishop of Canterbury. In 1807 Addington Place, near Croydon, was acquired as his summer home. Three Cabinet Ministers – the Earl of Liverpool who was then Prime Minister, Viscount Melville and Viscount Sidmouth – also had Surrey residences in 1815, at Combe House near Kingston, at Wimbledon, and the Ranger's House in Richmond Park respectively. The King's representative in Surrey was George, 4th Viscount Midleton, Lord Lieutenant of the county. He was an Irish peer with large estates in County Cork and a mansion called Peper-Harow near Godalming.

Thames to the dirty town of Brentford on the opposite side. Alas, in 1815 the ailing monarch was confined to Windsor Castle.

One of the King's sons, the Duke of York, maintained a country residence at Oatlands, near Weybridge. On 6 August 1815 the Duke,

... on coming out of a shower bath at his seat at Oatlands, fell, on account of the slippery state of the oil-cloth and broke the large bone of his left arm. Surgeons were sent express from London, who put the displaced parts into their natural position.

The period has been called the age of elegance, but it was far from elegant for the Surrey farm-worker who found himself facing problems which were beyond his understanding, and which were largely due to agri-

8. Frederick Augustus, Duke of York and Albany, KG (1763–1827), second son of George III, was noted for his kindly manners and generous nature. In 1791 his marriage was arranged with the daughter of the King of Prussia. The couple soon separated, and the Duchess retired to Oatlands, where she amused herself with pet dogs.

9. Robert, second Earl of Liverpool, first entered Parliament in 1790, becoming Prime Minister and chief of a purely Tory ministry in 1812. In 1815 his government decided on St Helena as the defeated Napoleon's place of exile.

10. Clandon Park, near Guildford, the magnificent home of Thomas, Earl of Onslow.

cultural policies in which, because of outworn electoral practices, his views were not sought. The traditional electoral system was wide open to abuse and had failed to adjust to the changing structure of life in the early nineteenth century.

The key issue was franchise. 'Surrey returns fourteen members to Parliament; two for the county, and two for each of the boroughs of Southwark, Guildford, Reigate, Haslemere, Blechingley and Gatton.' The right to vote for the two Members for the county normally belonged to all freeholders whose land brought in at least forty shillings annually. The county polls were taken at Guildford, and all the speeches, and the nomination of candidates, and the announcement of successful members duly elected were made from a platform set up in the open. The law allowed polling to continue for a fortnight. Candidates had the burden of paying the travelling expenses of voters to come to the polls, and also their board and lodgings in Guildford. As a certain amount of bribery was usually involved, elections could prove ruinous to the contestants.

The last general election had been held in 1812. In 1815 the M.P.s for the county were George Holme Sumner of Hatchlands, near Guildford, and Samuel Thornton who belonged to a famous Clapham family and was elder brother of the M.P. for Southwark. He was a Director of the Bank of England and a Governor of the Russia Company.

In the various boroughs the right to vote was absurdly limited, and some were thoroughly 'rotten'. Only half the district and population of Guildford possessed authority to vote, and the town was heavily influenced by the Onslow family of near-by Clandon Park. In 1815 the two M.P.s were the Hon. Thomas Cranley Onslow, and Arthur Onslow, serjeant-at-law, of Send Grove. The former was second son of Thomas, 2nd Earl of Onslow. The Earl, described as 'beneath the middle stature, and destitute of any elegance of grace', was a noted player of practical jokes. His other passion was driving four-in-hand, which inspired the following verse:

> What can Tommy O do?
> Why, drive a chaise and two.
> Can little Tommy do no more?
> Yes, drive a coach and four.

Blechingley and Reigate were described as Burgage or Burgage Tenure boroughs. The burgage was a feudal rental of land, and the number of voters in these towns was determined by the number of burgage holdings. So if a few individuals could buy up most of these burgage holdings they would gain a major influence over the voting. Once there had been about 130 voters in Blechingley, but the number that now attended elections was rarely more than ten.

In Reigate nearly all the 200 or so burgage freeholds were the property of the Earl of Hardwicke and Earl Somers, who could thus nominate any candidate they pleased. Lord Somers owned the mansion called Reigate Priory, and in 1815 the town's M.P.s were his eldest son the Hon. John Somers Cocks, and his cousin James Cocks, a London banker.

But most rotten of all the boroughs was undoubtedly Gatton, where there was just one voter for two seats. The six vote-entitled houses in this minute borough belonged to Sir Mark Wood, Bt., a Scotsman who had prospered in India as chief engineer of Bengal, and had bought himself Gatton Park. He occupied one of these six houses himself and let out the other five by the week. Since he alone paid the local rates he was the only person entitled to vote in this borough, and could thus vote himself and the other candidate into Parliament. Of Sir Mark it was said that he united in himself 'the functions of Member of Parliament, Magistrate, Churchwarden, Overseer, Surveyor of Highways, and Collector of Taxes' – since being the only freeholder in Gatton, he alone could act as parish officer.

In Southwark the right to vote belonged to 'the

B

inhabitants paying scot and lot [church and poor rates], amounting to about 3,200' out of a population of over 70,000. In 1815 there occurred a by-election on the death of one of the members, Henry Thornton. It commenced on 11 February and the hustings were erected opposite the Town Hall. A rich brewer, Charles Barclay, won the seat (the polling figures gave him a majority of 187 over his opponent, W.J. Burdett, brother of the M.P. for Westminster).

On Tuesday 28 February, Mr Barclay and some of his supporters were to dine at the Horns tavern at Kennington after the ceremony of 'chairing' the new member. This involved parading the boundaries of the Borough and meeting well-wishers. To begin with, all went smoothly, but when the new M.P. arrived at the Obelisk in St George's Fields he was met by a mob of several thousand of 'the lower orders of people', who threatened him and cried, 'No Corn Laws – No Barclay!' Apparently it was rumoured that Mr Barclay had voted in favour of the hated Corn laws.

Then:

the mob, collecting strength as it went forward, proceeded to acts of more determined hostility, and showers of mud, stones, and other missiles were poured upon Mr Barclay and his friends, who in consequence, were under the necessity of quickening their pace; but still the mob kept pace with them till they came into Blackman Street.

Here they were attacked by another mob, and both Barclay and his carriage were soon covered with filth. His friends were unhorsed and the windows of supporters broken. Soon he found himself in real danger. The magistrates were called upon to give armed protection. They contacted the Secretary of State, and remarkably promptly two troops of horse were sent down to the Horns tavern. In due course order was restored, and Barclay and friends calmly sat down to dinner as planned.

While the Corn Bill (passed on 20 March) was going through Parliament, reports were spread about that the new regulations would artificially cause a great rise in the price of corn, and thus of bread, which would disastrously affect the poor. Among the petitions of protest sent to Parliament were some from Southwark (9,650 signatures), Tooting and Croydon, which were presented on Monday 6 March. Passions ran high:

The words 'No Corn Bill' are now conspicuously chalked upon the walls in various parts of the town, and much ferment seems to prevail on the subject of the Resolutions now in progress through the House of Commons. Government are taking precautionary measures. . . . Thursday, the two Regiments of Life Guards were under orders the whole of the day, to be ready at a moment's notice.

Reasons for local unrest will become more apparent in the next chapter. It was fairly common to call in the soldiery to deal with civil rioting at this period. The old county force was the militia, of 800 men theoretically, raised by ballot – the price of exemption was £10 if one's name came up. The original uniform consisted of a long red coat, a long waistcoat, red breeches, and white gaiters. The skirts of the coat were made to hook back to reveal the colours of the facings of the regiment, as well as the bottom of the long red waistcoat. Up to 1759 the hair was powdered and tied up in a queue behind; thereafter the men were supplied with false queues. Despite the fine uniforms and cheap beer, great difficulty was experienced in getting the Southwark quota of the regiment complete. The men absconded as soon as they were enrolled and received some pay; it was almost impossible to find them two days later.

At the threat of war with revolutionary France in 1792, the militia was embodied as a full-time regiment, instead of a part-time defence force, and it thus became known as the 'regular' militia. It was soon implemented by several volunteer forces raised privately.

In 1797 the Surrey Militia was organized as two regiments, called the 1st Surrey and the 2nd Surrey. When the King reviewed the Surrey volunteers and yeomanry on Wimbledon Common in July 1799, they totalled 676 cavalry and 1,958 infantry or foot soldiers for the defence of the realm. Besides Lord Leslie's Surrey Yeomanry (253), the cavalry included the Richmond Yeomanry (80) and the Wandsworth Volunteers (25); the infantry included volunteer companies from Mortlake (42), Clapham (120) and Camberwell. About this time there were also the Croydon Cavalry, Guildford and Blackheath Cavalry, Woking Cavalry, Clapham Cavalry, Godley or Egham Cavalry, Lambeth Cavalry, Wimbledon Light Horse, and Southwark Cavalry.

Meanwhile, in 1804, the Surrey Militia received the title of a Royal regiment, and assumed blue facings. A man enlisting in the regular militia received a 10-guinea bounty, and if from there he enlisted into the regular army he would receive another 10 guineas for

11. The Surrey Yeomanry presented a splendid appearance: the uniform was light blue with scarlet cuffs, scarlet collar and shoulder-wings, black bearskin crested cavalry helmet with scarlet plumes, white breeches and black top-boots. Buttons and lace were silver.

seven years' service, or 14 guineas for an unlimited term – a very princely sum in those days. So it was that men wearing Surrey Militia jackets, yet fighting in the ranks of the Guards, could be seen on the field of Waterloo.

In 1809 a 'local' militia was also formed, using the patriotic services of men who could not enlist full-time but were available for local defence. In 1812 the local militia of about 5,000 men comprised five regiments

12. The semaphore telegraph tower in Newington. During recent wars the Admiralty always had up-to-date information of foreign ship movements. Credit for the quick passage of naval intelligence must be given to the semaphore stations linking Portsmouth with the Admiralty. A series of stations 5 to 10 miles apart was built on high ground at Pewley Down near Guildford, Chatley Heath, Hinchley Wood, Coombe Hill, Putney Heath, and else-where. The signalling system used two semaphore arms, somewhat like railway signals. Watch was kept during daylight. With a telescope sighted on the next station to follow the rapid movement of the arms there, an instruction could be passed along the line from Portsmouth to London in less than a minute!

with headquarters at Guildford, Kingston, Croydon, Putney and Clapham.

On Napoleon's abdication in 1814 the local militia was disbanded and the regular militia was disembodied, though the yeomanry cavalry remained. And on Napoleon's return from Elba the regular militia was again called out, but was disembodied after the victory at Waterloo put an end to the foreign threat.

So that command of the Militia, Yeomanry and Volunteers might be in the hands of persons keenly interested in the defence of Surrey, property qualifi-cations – besides other stipulations as to social position (which were left to the discretion of the Lord Lieu-tenant) – were required at the following rates: a colonel had to possess an estate of the yearly value of £1,000, or to be heir-apparent of a person with an estate of a yearly value of £2,000; a lieutenant-colonel needed about two-thirds of this fortune; majors and captains needed an estate of £200 per annum, or to be the younger son of a parent with an estate of £600, or heir-apparent of a person with an estate worth £400 yearly.

It is further evidence of their strong influence in the county, that for many years members of the Onslow family held commands in the local regiments. In late 1815 the newly disembodied 2nd Royal Surrey Militia was commanded by Colonel the Hon. Thomas Cranley Onslow, MP, with headquarters at Guildford. The headquarters of the 1st Royal Surrey were at Kingston; its colonel was Lord Grantley, of Green Place, Wonersh.

3. Poverty and philanthropy

Early in 1815 Mr Serjeant Onslow rose in the House to present a petition from the Mayor, Corporation, and inhabitants of Guildford against the renewal of the property tax. He stated that these petitioners had cheerfully borne the tax during the war, but conceived that they were now all entitled to exemption from this burden. The property tax was repealed.

By the end of February a new schedule of taxes was published. These were wide-spread and imposed even heavier taxation on some. The following extract shows the odd nature of these payments – how foolish, people muttered, to have complained about the old taxes!

HOUSES. For every inhabited house or tenement of the yearly valued rent of £5 and under £20, a rate of 2s. in the pound.

SERVANTS. Every person keeping male servants, to pay each as follows: for one such servant, if not in livery, £4. 10s., for one, if in livery, £5. 10s. And if the master be a bachelor, a further sum of £5.

HORSES. On 1 horse, £5; 2 horses, £8; 3 horses, £9. And if the proprietor be a bachelor, £5 per cent additional on the amount so chargeable.

CARRIAGES. On carriages with four wheels, by every person keeping them, £21. And for every additional body to be successively used on the same carriage or pair of wheels, £11. And if the owner be a bachelor, £50 per cent additional.

DOGS. For every greyhound, pointer, setting-dog, or spaniel, each £1. 10s. For every hound, lurcher, or terrier, each £1.

The discrimination against bachelors brought at least one quick result. In April 1815 the marriage at Croydon was reported of Mr Wheelright, aged 66, to Miss Elizabeth Goodman, of Mitcham, aged 58, after a courtship of 39 years. 'It is a well known fact, that the match was finally settled in haste, in consequence of the proposed increase of assessed taxes on bachelors.'

The new taxes would chiefly affect the moderately well-off, but the poorest classes were finding the prices of everything beyond their slender means; unrest among unemployed labourers had encouraged rioting. The majority of working-class people in Surrey were rurally-orientated despite the influence of the metropolis. Small freeholders or yeomen and their labourers were, of course, very much at the mercy of price levels. Peasants and yeomen now began to find themselves at starvation level through inexplicable causes: local taxation, Government policy, foreign wars – all three could assail them at one time. On top of this they found their common lands disappearing. The rash of land enclosure Acts referred to in Chapter 2, based on the principle of gathering common lands and small uneconomic strips into larger holdings, had been causing acute distress for a long time. In many cases the disappearance of the commons had left the smaller men with no stake in the soil.

Despite the successful harvest of 1815, a report of early December stated:

The continuing depression of the corn market operates so

severely on the landed interest, that scarce a parish in any county but is suffering under calamitous and increasing privations, the whole of which are justly ascribed to the last year's superfluous importation of foreign grain.

Prices of bread and flour were extortionate, due to artificial regulation. Added to this the recent dry weather had allowed early completion of many winter agricultural tasks, so that labourers were threatened with unemployment. Many had large families depending on their wages. Government statistics reported the following weekly wages paid in 1815, but shortage of work caused many a family man to accept less: carpenters 25s.; bricklayers 22s.; plumbers 21s.; shoemakers 16s.; labourers 15s.

Seldom in Surrey's history had farm labourers and yeomen been so badly off. Bread and cheese washed down with beer became the staple diet. Increasingly rarely did they see meat. The prices of essentials show how difficult it was for a man earning less than £1 weekly to feed and clothe his family adequately:

Bread, 2½d. per lb.	Suit of clothes, £2. 7s.
Meat, 1s. 4d. per lb.	Stockings, 2s. 1½d. per pair.
Butter, 10½d. per lb.	Linen for shirts, 1s. per yard.
Cheese, 5½d. per lb.	Hats, 3s. each.

Shoes, 4s. 6d. per pair.

The labourers' sufferings were aggravated by the strong measures for enforcing game laws. Men whose families stole turnips to relieve their hunger, and who saw pheasants, partridges and hares swarming in woods around them, could not resist the temptation of creeping out at night with a gun and net to fill the pot. In January 1815 John Cooke was taken before the magistrates at Epsom. It appeared that he and three other men were caught in a park near Epsom by Hunt, the gamekeeper; a bag in their possession containing 20 hares and 8 pheasants. 'Hunt, with the assistance of three constables, succeeded in handcuffing the four poachers, and lodged them in the watch-house, from whence, with the assistance of their accomplices outside they effected their escape.' A constable, having received private information, apprehended Cooke at a public house. The charge having been proved against Cooke, he was fined £30, a sum equal to about 8 months' wages, and in default of payment committed for three months to prison.

Many farm labourers turned to factory work to feed their families. The end of the war not only brought a trade recession, but unemployment grew when thousands of ex-soldiers and sailors from the Napoleonic wars flooded the market. The class below the yeomen – cottagers and squatters – were the worst hit by the enclosure of lands. A large number of destitute persons had to be maintained by the county. A fairly recent survey showed that 5,268 poor were maintained in workhouses at an expense of £75,000; the number of persons maintained out of workhouses at the same time was 37,745, at a cost of £59,000.

Sometimes workhouse labour was hired out. An advertisement of 1815 read:

To Workhouse Masters. To let at Walton-on-Thames, Surrey, a manufactory in the woollen, hemp and flax line, established in the Workhouse of that parish. . . . The vestry give notice that they will be ready to receive proposals in writing. . . . The contractor must engage to carry on the present manufactory. There are at present about 50 spinning wheels. The poor to be humanely treated, victualled, clothed, and kept constantly clean. . . .

It was announced that the bill of fare for Wandsworth Workhouse was in future to be as follows:

Sundays: Milk porridge, 8 oz. of beef with vegetables, and two pints of beer.
Mondays: Porridge, pease soup, and two pints of beer.
Tuesdays: Porridge, half a quartern loaf, 8 oz. of beef and vegetables, and two pints of beer.
Wednesdays: Milk porridge, pease soup, quarter pound of butter or half pound of cheese, and two pints of beer.
Thursdays: Porridge, half a quartern loaf, 1 lb. of suet pudding, and two pints of beer.
Fridays: Milk porridge, 8 oz. of beef with vegetables, and two pints of beer.
Saturdays: Porridge, half a quartern loaf, quarter pound of butter or half pound of cheese, and two pints of beer.

An easy escape for the poor from the harsh reality of their lives was cheap alcohol. At this time the drinking of gross amounts of gin had become a national scandal. In Surrey this year a committee of magistrates was appointed

. . . to consider the great increase in the number of shops for the sale of gin and other spirituous liquors, and to report their opinion of the consequences of such increase, and the most efficient means of suppressing and regulating the same. . . .

The report continued:

It is a notorious fact, that many of the inferior classes of people who formerly brewed their own small or table beer, have long since ceased to do so, and are for the most part become frequenters of the gin-shop. It is well known too, that the habit of drinking spirits rapidly grows. . . . He who sits for hours fuddling over his pot of beer is generally rendered dull and senseless; whilst he who quickly tosses off his drams of gin or whiskey, is rendered furious and fit for any active wickedness.

– one reason for the increase in crime.

Yet despite this picture of misery, among the humbler classes there could also be much simple happiness. The life of village children, playing in the hedges and thickets, was wholesome and natural, as Bewick, Wordsworth and Cobbett recorded.

The Church provided a measure of help and satisfaction to many villagers, but often the profession of clergyman had become no more than a way of life for the sons of privileged families. The parson could hunt with the squire, get drunk or gamble with the gentry, farm his glebe, indulge his hobbies – intellectual or otherwise. The Established Church parson delivered as his sermon a logical, reasonable theological essay, spoken in a perfectly level tone with an upper-class accent. God knows that it could be boring! Such sermons were often totally incomprehensible to the poor and uneducated of Surrey.

Conditions were ripe for the encouragement of any dissenters (nonconformists) whose message could make Christianity more meaningful to the working classes. The last decade had seen John Wesley's movement and similar dissenting bodies grow. The squires had no

13. The octagonal Surrey Chapel in Blackfriars Road was founded by Revd. Rowland Hill, who was minister of a congregation of Calvinistic Methodists here for over fifty years. He was 'followed by the most crowded audiences, chiefly composed of the lower classes of society', though many wealthy people also attended regularly. This chapel was opened in 1783 at a cost of about £5,000. The first Sunday school in London was established here.

love for these half-starved and shabbily-dressed preachers, and parsons of the Established Church were annoyed to witness the peace of their parishes disturbed by zealous nonconformists.

In 1813 John Venn died. Rector of Clapham for 21 years, an original founder of the Church Missionary Society and a strong opponent of the slave-trade, he had gathered in his parish a motley collection of Evangelicals – dissenters, lawyers, M.P.s, businessmen – who became known as the Clapham Sect. Among them was William Wilberforce, whose continued efforts had won the Act of 1807 abolishing the British slave-trade. For a while he had lived at Broomfield, on the southwest side of Clapham Common, but by 1815 had moved elsewhere.

Another of this group was Henry Thornton, of Battersea Rise, who died in 1815. A wealthy banker, he had been M.P. for Southwark since 1782 (though always refusing to pay the guinea customarily expected to reward each elector's vote). He supported Roman Catholic emancipation, was a leading member of the Church Missionary Society and the British and Foreign Bible Society, devoted a third of his £9,000 yearly income to charity, and won great respect for his intelligence and integrity.

In Clapham High Street lived Zachary Macaulay, father of the famous historian, Thomas Babington Macaulay. After Sierra Leone was founded to provide a centre of civilization for the African races, he was appointed Governor in 1793, and against heavy odds succeeded in raising the colony to a reasonable state of prosperity. By 1815 he was a very prosperous merchant, and was editor of the *Christian Observer*, the newspaper of the Clapham Sect.

This group, the 'Saints' as they were sneeringly called, fought and won many battles. They forced the Church to pay a reasonable stipend to curates; the printing and free circulation of Bibles came by their efforts. Through their pressure the King issued a proclamation condemning sabbath-breaking, blasphemy, drunkenness, obscene literature and immoral amusements. They did much to lessen the moral apathy of their day.

Agitation against the Corn Bill was matched by industrial unrest. In the North, mechanization of industries, causing unemployment, had raised widespread protest, and produced the Luddite machine-breaking movement. The Luddite Movement later spread southwards, causing something approaching popular insurrection. From the hunger, strife, and bloody pavements one outstanding figure emerged – William Cobbett.

Cobbett was born at Farnham in 1762. He spent his boyhood scaring birds from growing crops until, at an early age, he taught himself to drive a team and could take over the family ploughing. His father taught him reading, writing and arithmetic in the winter evenings. He left home at the age of eleven and found work at Kew Gardens. There he worked as clerk until he joined the army. Cobbett rose to the rank of sergeant-major, served in North America, bought his discharge in the States, and in 1800 returned to England.

In 1809 a mutiny broke out among the local militia. Cobbett's *Political Register* (which he published for

thirty-three years) commented strongly on the punishment inflicted on these civilian-soldiers. He was arrested for this criticism of the law, sentenced to two years in prison, and viciously forced to pay a huge fine of £1,000. After this term in gaol he became more anti-establishment than ever. It was from his comments and pamphlets that the true nature of village life could be seen. His reports on the hardships suffered by small

14. William Wilberforce, the great philanthropist.

15. William Cobbett was an honest but fiery porcupine, a thorn in the flesh of authority, who aimed to make his own county, Surrey, and England better places to live in.

farmers helped social workers to build up a picture of rural problems. He hated those who used wealth or position improperly.

Although a great amount of hunger and misery appears in reports by people like Cobbett, bad times were not always the rule. At the time of their victory over Napoleon the English did not look like people accustomed to go hungry. The bitterness of their resentment when they did, came from their sense that this was something outside the course of nature.

Many of the labourers from parishes near London – Vauxhall, Battersea, Clapham, Wandsworth – were huge fellows with massive shoulders and ruddy faces, quite different from the tradition picture of pallid Continentals. For all its harshness and injustice, these simple folk thought there was no country like their own. At a farm feast or in village alehouses an artless chorus which showed their love of England's free traditions would ring out, giving warning to foreigners who relied on strength:

> The race is not always got
>   By them wot strive and for it run,
> Nor the battel to them people
>   Wot's got the longest gun.

4. Agriculture and rural life

[On 2 May] . . . a most alarming storm took place at Addington, near Croydon. A water-spout descended on the hill, and burst about a mile above it. The water poured in torrents and rushing into the valley formed a stream fifty feet wide. It took its way with irresistible force through the village, forced open the doors, and carried away the furniture of the habitations. . . . This deluge accompanied by thunder and lightning continued for upwards of two hours.

Despite this phenomenon, the early months of 1815 were mild enough for it to be said: 'The spring crops – oats, barley, beans, pease, seeds, are universally most luxuriant and promising.' By July the wheat crop was expected to be abundant, and in early September the greater part of the harvest was gathered: 'The new wheats already sent to market have presented a dry and fine sample. Beans are an universal great crop; barley and oats about, or somewhat above, an average.' Turnips, swedes and hops suffered, but for the most part the abundant autumn gathering justified the villagers in singing their Harvest Home songs with heartfelt feeling.

A survey of the period remarked:

In regard to agricultural improvements Surrey may be considered as behind many other districts of Great Britain. The arable land far exceeds the proportion of pasture . . . The drill husbandry has not found many followers in Surrey, except in the west part of the county, about Bagshot, Esher, Send, Cobham and Ripley, where it is very general. The climate of Surrey seems to be less favourable to oats than to wheat or barley. . . . Garden pease and beans are cultivated in the immediate neighbourhood of the metropolis.

Turnips had been raised in Surrey as long as in any other district. Cabbages were grown chiefly near London, as were carrots, which fetched about £16 to £24 an acre. Potatoes were not a common crop, except at Mitcham, Tooting, Streatham and Norwood. 'The tops are frequently cut by the cow-keepers to be given to cattle when other food becomes scarce.' Hops were widely cultivated around Farnham, 'where they

16. Tooting in 1815: 'The land is principally arable.' Large areas now built over were then still very rural.

occupy about 900 acres, the produce of which fetches a higher price than that of any other hop-district in the kingdom'.

The area of gardens raising vegetables for the London market totalled about 3,500 acres, and some Surrey gardens were particularly distinguished for asparagus, especially at Mortlake, East Sheen and Battersea.

Above two hundred and sixty acres of land in the parish of Battersea (including somewhat more than a hundred in the common fields) are occupied by the market gardeners. These gardeners employ, in the summer season, a considerable number of labourers. . . . The wages of the men are from ten to twelve, of the women from five to seven shillings, by the week. Most of the women travel on foot from Shropshire and North Wales in the spring; and, as they live at a very cheap rate, many of them return to their own country much richer than when they left it.

'Surrey has a much smaller proportion of grass-land than most other counties in England'; most of this lay along the banks of the Thames, in the north-west, along the Mole near Cobham, and the Wey near Godalming.

Surrey seemingly had no particular breed of cattle it could call its own. The cows supplying London with milk were almost exclusively of the short-horned, or Holderness breed. Further from the city other breeds were kept by the gentry and farmers. 'Most of the cattle fattened for the butcher in Surrey are in the hands of the great distillers in the vicinity of London. . . . Many of the gentlemen and farmers also occasionally fatten a few oxen; but none of them to such an extent as Mr Adam of Mount Nod, or Mr Coles of Norbury.' Mr Adam's buildings could house 600 cattle at a time.

Large numbers of sheep were kept in central and western Surrey, but only recently had much attention been paid to improved breeding. Commonest were the South Down, Wiltshire and Dorsetshire breeds, though another type survived in the western heaths: 'A pure heath sheep is a remarkably ugly creature, with very large horns.'

Yeomen farmers were not nearly so numerous as in neighbouring Kent, but around Guildford and in parts of the Weald there were several worth between £200 and £400 a year. 'The size of farms also in Surrey may be considered as rather small than large', the largest being about 1,600 acres, and a few others between 600 and 1,200 acres; 'but the most common size is from 200 to 300'. In fact one observer considered 170 acres about the average size in the county.

In regard to the farm-houses, a striking difference appears in different districts. In the Vale, or Weald, of Surrey, they are too often mean and ruinous. . . . In the other parts of the county they are in general sufficiently large and convenient, in good repair, and kept neat and clean. The oldest are built entirely of brick, and mostly covered with large heavy slate-stone; and many are constructed of a framing of wood lathed and plastered, or rough-cast. . . . The cottages are in general sufficiently large and convenient for the class of persons by whom they are occupied; and a small piece of ground for growing vegetables is commonly attached to them.

Rural hamlets, living by agriculture, were often tightly-knit self-supporting communities. Even the poorest normally found enough food to carry them through bad periods. It was an organic way of life which had evolved among peasants with their roots in the soil: it

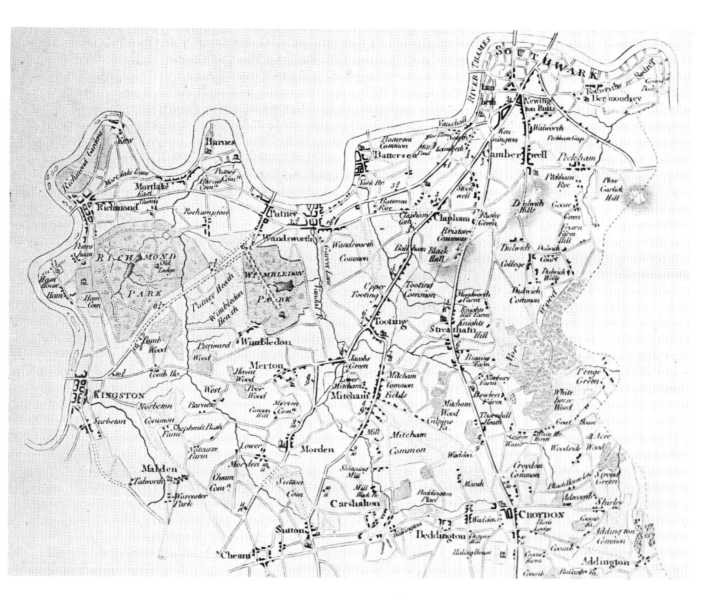

A map of around 1815 showing some of the wide stretches of common land, many of which still survive in south London – in Clapham, Wandsworth, Wimbledon, Tooting, Mitcham and elsewhere. In the south centre is Sutton: 'The inhabitants have a right of turning out their cattle upon Sutton and Bonhill commons in this parish, during a certain part of the year.'

had been good enough for their fathers and so it was a good enough way of life for them, despite talk in the bigger towns of changes and unemployment. But change was here to stay, and the old peasant life-style was to be ever more radically altered by new agricultural methods and not least by the gradual disappearance of the commons, as already referred to in Chapters 2 and 3. Common lands historically belonging to villagers remained open to all. Pigs and cattle grazed there; birds and rabbits were trapped for the pot; field fruits and wood for fuel were available for any in need. Ox-drawn ploughs, siring bulls and rams served as communal aids which could be used by all parishioners in turn. Often a man was allowed to tether one horse or cow on the common, and also graze one sheep. Those with surplus eggs, butter, poultry or young beasts to sell or exchange went to market each week; across the road stood the church and at least one public house. Itinerant traders laid out their goods on a patch of ground which was traditionally theirs for the day.

Even in the worst times the diet of the Surrey working classes had never fallen to the dreadful level of many parts of Europe where starvation and typhus slaughtered thousands. Now, where before the war farm workers had enjoyed meat almost daily, there had been a big falling-off in protein, but the diet was still well above the level of Continental peasants who lived part of the year on roots.

The field labourer's wear was a straw hat and a round smock-frock, usually white, worn over doublet, breeches and leggings. His cottage of local material blended with its surrounding. Simple furniture, oak and elm settles flanking rough-hewn tables thick enough to chop up a side of beef, took up most of the spare space. On Sundays the Surrey lanes were gay with servant maids showing their new dresses, silk gowns and fancy petticoats.

Some plants commonly found growing in the countryside were recorded:

The most curious are Birds-foot, in the fields near Cobham. Wild Rue, on Leith Hill. Thorow-wax, near Croydon. Maiden Pinks, near Esher. Blue sweet-smelling Toad-flax, in the hedges near Farnham. Self-heal near Kingston. Buckthorn, in the hedges near Farnham. And on the Downs near Dorking are wild black cherries, from which the inhabitants make wine little inferior to French claret.

'It is conceived, that a greater quantity of land is employed in raising physical plants in this county than in any other in England.' Among those grown by James Moore of Mitcham were:

Peppermint. Its virtues are that of being greatly stomachic and carminative.

Angelica. It is often sold to confectioners for sweetmeats; as a confection it is nicely warming but the most agreeable imaginable. It is good to expel wind and strengthen the stomach.

Hyssop. This plant is considered by some extremely grateful to the smell; it is usually recommended against asthmas, coughs, and all disorders of the breast and lungs whether boiled in broths or otherwise.

Lavender. The oil is sold to perfumers and chemists at forty shillings per pound.

There was a curious custom of inheritance at Richmond: 'lands in this manor are held by the rod, or copy of court-roll, and descend to the youngest son; or in default of sons, to the youngest daughter. The same customs prevail in the manors of Petersham and Ham.'

Increasing mobility and the spread of education were beginning to modify the old Surrey dialects and erode the range of proverbs once in daily use. Traditional sayings were also losing their credibility, though many were still commonly heard. One popular saying was: 'As far the sun shines into the house on Candlemas day [2 February], so far will the snow drive in before the winter is out.' A fine Easter Day was supposed to be followed by 'plenty of grass, but little good hay'. A fine bark-harvest (fine weather for getting in the bark after the oak 'flawing'* was done) indicated fine weather for getting in the crop harvest. Thus a farmer might say: 'I expect we shall have a shuckish [showery] time at harvest. We had it so at bark-harvest, and they generally follow one another.' This type of phrase in a strong local accent might well bring the proceedings before, say, a bench of magistrates to a full stop until a translation was given.

There was a persistent prejudice against thunder early in the year, hence the saying: 'Early thunder, late hunger.' Agricultural families had a proverb: 'When the cuckoo comes to a bare thorn, then there's likely to be plenty of corn.' Thus a late spring was thought to predict a fruitful harvest.

The direction from which the wind blew on any of the quarter-days was significant. It was thought that the wind would remain in much the same direction for the three months until the next quarter-day. (A similar

*flawing – cracking of the bark under winter conditions.

prediction involved Kingston Fair Day, occurring on 13 November.) When there was not a glimmer of moonlight at Christmas – 'A dark Christmas makes a heavy wheatsheaf' – this signified a good harvest the next year.

'Deaf as a beetle' had nothing to do with an insect, but meant the same as 'Deaf as a post' – beetle, or biddle, in Surrey was the name for a mallet or a post-shaped utensil for mashing potatoes or beating washing.

A number of old superstitions lingered on into the nineteenth century. It was believed by some that a cake baked on Good Friday would keep any length of time and not become mouldy.

18. Mitcham. 'About 250 acres are occupied by the physic gardeners, who cultivate lavender, wormwood, camomile, aniseed, rhubarb, liquorice and many other medicinal plants, in great abundance; but principally peppermint, of which there are above 100 acres. The demand for this herb is not confined to the apothecaries' shops, it being much used in making a cordial well-known to the dram-drinkers.'

19. The wooden toll bridge at Putney. 'Smelts are caught here in great abundance in the months of March and April, and are esteemed very fine. The salmon fishery is not very productive, but the fish are of very good quality, and sell for a high price. Small flounders, shad, roach, dace, barbel, eels and gudgeons, may be reckoned also among the produce of the fisheries here. One or two sturgeons are generally taken in the course of a year; and sometimes, though rarely, a porpus.'

To cure a child of whooping-cough a nut was hollowed out and a live spider put inside. The nut was then hung by a string round the child's neck. When the spider died the infection was supposed to die with it.

It was believed among country folk that the moss or 'comb' (pronounced *coom*) which collects on church bells could be used as a cure for shingles – a painful disease running along a nerve. This moss was scraped off the bells and firmly rubbed into the patient's skin, despite the yells.

Some explanation is needed for the expression: 'Go on a pig to Putney!' 'Pig' is an old word for basin or bowl. Putney was a common starting place for journeys, and everybody went to Putney by water. Thus 'Go on a pig to Putney!' was like saying 'Go to Putney in a bowl', or, more simply, 'Go and get drowned!'

5. A tour of the towns

On the 21st of September we embarked on the ship *Recovery* at Millbank and was immediately under weigh, all oars in motion.

Arriving on the southern coast, consulted our charts, and found the land was called Surrey, and determined it was a corruption of Sore-eye, a complaint, we presumed, the inhabitants were remarkable for enduring. . . .

We proceeded slowly along its banks and passed Cleaver's soap manufactory, situate on a marshy tract. This building afforded us some idea of the inhabitants – whom we concluded were clean.

Arrived at Battersea bridge, clock striking ten. Observed some people spitting from the bridge into the water, others lolling carelessly and whistling, others idling their lazy lengths upon an old wall, and wandering a vacant stare upon us: concluded, from ocular demonstration, that the inhabitants of Sore-eye were idolent.

Of course the general appearance of the county in 1815 could not be judged merely from a quick glance at the south bank of the Thames! Southwark, Lambeth, Battersea and Wandsworth lay in the most thickly populated corner of Surrey – and the most commercially and industrially important. But they were far more closely tied to London than to the rest of the county's 'fifteen market towns and boroughs', and certainly offered no hint of the rural beauties that lay beyond.

Contemporary accounts from around 1815 help to

21. The Surrey Institution, in Blackfriars Road, was 'one of those useful establishments recently formed in the Metropolis for the diffusion of science. Its object comprises a series of lectures, extensive library, and reading-rooms, a chemical laboratory, and philosophical apparatus.' The membership fee was 50 guineas.

give us a picture of the major settlements as we move away from the metropolis. First Southwark itself: 'This borough, which is commonly considered as the capital of Surrey, is itself but a suburb and appendage to the prodigious metropolis of the British empire.' A teaming warren of streets devoted to commerce and industry, it had many notable buildings. The Borough Market near St Saviour's Church (now Southwark Cathedral) was 'a spacious area, surrounded with stalls and other conveniences for the sale of various kinds of provisions, especially vegetables, the principal market for flesh being on the west side of the Borough High Street'.

On the east side of Blackman Street was the Marshalsea, notorious as a debtors' prison. 'To this place also persons guilty of piracies, and other offences on the high seas, are committed, though the offenders are tried at the Old Bailey.' In Union Street was Union Hall, 'a handsome structure, appropriated to the purposes of a police office; and at the south-east end of Blackman Street, in Horsemonger Lane, is the County Gaol and House of Correction for Surrey'. The 'clink', an old prison for detaining rowdy breakers of the peace, still existed and was described as 'a filthy, noisome dungeon'.

A little farther out was the smart suburb of Clapham (population about 5,000):

... the village consists of many handsome houses, surrounding a common, that commands many pleasing views. This common, about the commencement of the present reign, was little better than a morass, and the roads were almost impassable. The latter are now in an excellent state; and the common so beautifully planted with trees, that it has the appearance of a park. These improvements were effected by a subscription of the inhabitants.

Richmond (population about 5,200)

is ... perhaps the finest village in the British dominions. ... At Marsh Gate, nine almshouses were erected and endowed by Mr and Mrs Houblon, in 1758, for maiden women; they are allowed about four shillings and ninepence *per* week, and firing; also a new gown yearly. The charity school is in George Street, where thirty-four boys and

thirty-four girls are educated; they are instructed in the principles of the Christian religion, and the boys are taught to read, write, and cast accompts; and the girls to read, write, knit, mark, etc.

Mitcham's population was about 4,000:

A beautiful stream called the Wandle, remarkable for the pureness and transparency of its water, passes through it; upon which are mills for grinding corn, tobacco, logwood, etc.: and on the banks are some very convenient and pleasant grounds, for the purpose of bleaching and printing calico.

Kingston's population was about 4,000 and its chief trade hops and malt. The market was held on Saturdays, and there were three annual fairs –

. . . on Whit-Thursday and two following days for horses and toys; on the 2nd, 3rd and 4th of August for fruit, principally cherries and pedlary; and on the 13th of November for cattle of the Welch, Scotch and Irish breeds, and also hogs and sheep.

23. Croydon, 'a handsome market town'.

Carshalton was thought to stand 'on one of the most beautiful spots south of London, on which account it has many handsome houses; some built with such grandeur and expence, that they might be rather taken for the seats of the nobility than the country houses of citizens and merchants'.

At Ewell 'The market day is Thursday, and there are two fairs on May 12, and October 29. The town has a very romantic appearance, but nothing else very particular. . . .' In fact, contrary to this opinion, we have already seen that the town had gunpowder mills on the Hogsmill; and see the references to Nonsuch House and Ewell Castle in Chapter 7.

'Leatherhead, a small town, on a rising ground . . . had anciently a market, which has long been discontinued. It consists of four streets intersecting in the centre, and containing several good mansions.' And 'for delightfulness of situation, prospect, and healthfulness, very few places can vie with Leatherhead'.

Epsom's population was about 2,500. 'This town has been long famous for its mineral waters, tinctured with allum . . . and the salt made from them is famous throughout Europe, for their gently cleansing, cooling and purifying quality.'

It was probably much more famous already for the Derby and Oaks racing events held on the near-by Downs for the past thirty-five years.

The meal trade at Dorking is considerable. The market day is Thursday, which, for many ages, has been one of the greatest in England for poultry; it is likewise a good corn market . . . an incredible quantity of poultry is sold here, which are large and fine, and remarkable for having five

Croydon's population was nearly 6,000.

The present market, on Saturday, is chiefly for oats and oatmeal for London; there is also a good sale for wheat and barley; the fair on October 2, is much frequented by persons of both sexes from London, for walnuts, etc. The adjacent hills are well stored with wood, of which great quantities of charcoal are made for London.

A new town hall was recently built, suitable to receive the judges at the summer assizes.

24. Carshalton. 'The river Wandle passes through the parish, and being increased by other streams and several springs which rise there, forms a large sheet of remarkably clear water, in the centre of the village.' Along the river bank stood two paper-mills, two skinning-mills, and mills for grinding drugs and boring cannon.

claws. Frequently, about Christmas, capons are so large, as to weigh between seven and eight pounds out of their feathers.

The population was about 3,200.

Reigate borough's population was about 1,128. 'The neighbourhood abounds with fuller's earth, and medicinal plants and herbs.'
At Chertsey,

The charity-school was founded by Sir William Perkins, Kt., in the year 1725, for clothing and educating twenty-five poor boys, and the same number of poor girls, and instructing them in reading, writing, arithmetic, etc. The workhouse is commodious for the aged and infirm; the younger persons are employed in winding and spinning wool. In the town are five almshouses, under the management and care of the parish officers. There are four good annual fairs, on the first Monday in Lent for horses, cows, hogs and toys; May 14, for sheep and lambs, cows, horses, hogs and toys; August 6, for black cherries, hogs, horses, cows and toys; September 25 is a statute fair, for the hiring of servants of both sexes, and also for the sale of onions, hogs, horses, cows, toys, etc.

25. 'Dorking is a pleasant little market town. . . . The custom of Borough English prevails in this manor, that is, the youngest son is heir to a copyhold estate.' (See the system of inheritance in Richmond, described in Chapter 4).

26. Guildford. 'In its present state this may justly be considered one of the best inland towns of its size in the kingdom.'

With a population of about 3,000, 'Guildford, the county town of Surrey is large and well built. . . . It has a weekly market on Saturday, at which great quantities of corn are exposed for sale.' At summer assizes one court sat in the town hall, and the other in what used to be the Red Lion Inn. The gaol was rebuilt in stone in 1765. The town was governed by a corporation consisting of high steward, mayor, recorder, seven magistrates and about twenty bailiffs.

Bagshot, a very pleasant little town . . . is remarkable for the neatness of its inns, and the good accommodations they afford to travellers. . . . Formerly the whole tract of country round Bagshot, for near twenty miles, very much resembled an arid desert. The sheep bred upon it are small, but remarkably fine flavoured; and when well fatted, and in proper order, produce the sweetest mutton in the world; this induces many who pass through the town, to carry home some of the Bagshot mutton in their carriages.

Bagshot Park belonged to the Duke of Gloucester, one of the royal family.

Egham's population was about 2,800.

Here is a neat almshouse . . . for six men and six women, who must be sixty years of age, and have been parishioners of Egham twenty years, without having received any parochial relief. They have each annually a chaldron of coals, clothing and five pounds in money. The centre of this building is a good house for a schoolmaster, who has £40 a year and a chaldron of coals, (besides an allowance for an assistant) for the education of twenty poor boys of Egham.

Farnham's population was around 2,500. 'It consists of one principal street, running nearly east and west,

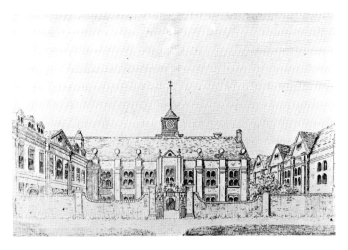

containing many excellent houses, and some smaller ones *branching off* to the north and south.' The town had three annual fairs, on Holy Thursday, 4 June, and 13 November, for horses, cattle, sheep and pigs.

So much for the Surrey towns in 1815, where formal education was so rare that the major schools deserved special comment. Charity schools, though few enough, were the only source of free education open to children whose parents did not keep them working at trades or on the land. Miss Bird's boarding-school for young ladies (see page 13) was definitely a preserve of the rich.

27. Dulwich College was established in 1619 by Edward Alleyne 'for a master, warden, four fellows, six poor brethren, and six sisters, twelve scholars, six assistants, and thirty out-members. . . . The statutes direct that the master and warden should be of the blood and surname of Alleyne; and for want of such, of his surname only.' Thus when William Allen, the master, died in 1805, he was succeeded by Thomas Allen; the warden was Launcelot Baugh Allen. 'The poor brethren and sisters must be sixty years of age at their admission, and unmarried. . . . The twelve poor scholars are to be six or eight years of age at their admission, and to be educated till they are eighteen: to be taught writing, reading, grammar, music, and good manners.'

6. Social concerns

In all the Surrey towns a pressing problem was the removal of garbage and keeping the streets clean. In early times house refuse was hurled straight out of doors and windows into the narrow crooked streets, where the tastiest pieces were fallen upon by stray dogs. By the seventeenth century certain places were set aside in towns as laystalls or temporary dumping places where anyone might dump refuse for collection by rakers. Each town ward had an unpaid scavenger to see that the law was obeyed. The mayor's accounts in the Guildford Hallwardens' books show entries from the mid-eighteenth century of sums of money, usually £6 per year, paid for cleaning the town.

Some years previous to 1815, a meeting held at Walton-on-Thames decided, among other matters, to let out the street dirt of the parish for the ensuing year. The dirt attracted a bid of thirty-three shillings for the Town and Commonside divisions. Until the last part of the eighteenth century the value of town filth had been largely unappreciated by farmers; it only took the activities of a few shrewd farmers to change that. It was found that, for example, coal ashes and cinders mixed with clay dried and hardened to a valuable building material. Now the value of hitherto neglected town refuse exceeded the cost of its removal; contractors were forced to pay for the privilege of removing it.

'Dust Ho!' shouted the dustman and rang his bell loudly and merrily to encourage the townsfolk to offer up their refuse. However, filth, as most trading commodities, had its ups and downs in value; by 1815 the sanitary authorities had once more to pay for removal, as the scavenging contractor 'was not prepared to do it for nothing'.

The clothes of dustmen in Southwark in the years around 1815 were probably much like those worn in London: the most usual features were fan-tail hats and spats. 'Dusty Bob, the parish dustman', in a coloured illustration, is shown wearing a red cap and fan-tail hat, a brown coat, blue waistcoat, shirt criss-crossed in blue, a white apron, red breeches, blue and white stockings and brown spats. He carries a bell, brush and shovel, and looks more ready for a leading rôle in a grand opera than for a dirty job of work.

Little was done, it seems, to protect the general public from airborne, waterborne or contagious diseases. A large number of Surrey hovels were 'mud without and wretchedness within'. The introduction of the iniquitous window-tax did a great service in removing extra mouths to feed! A smallish house with a door flanked by side windows attracted only small taxation. But one more window each side raised one's window-tax enormously, so a great many property-owners permanently boarded them up. In these airless dank conditions in Wandsworth and Lambeth many an artisan and his family lived and worked in one room. Such an environment was clinically ripe for the spread of consumption. There were few authentic cures; here is one tried in 1814:

To stew a Cock against Consumption. Cut him into six pieces and wash him clean. Then take prunes, currants, dates, raisins, sugar, three or four leaves of gold, cinnamon, ginger, nutmeg, and some maiden-hair chopped very small. Put all these aforesaid things into a flagon with a pint of muscadine. And boil them in a great brass pot of half a bushel. Stop the mouth of the flagon withal by a piece of paste and let it boil the space of twelve hours. Being well stewed, strain the liquor, and give it to the party to drink cold; two or three spoonfuls in the morning fasting and it shall help him. This is an approved medicine.

The newspapers were full of wordy advertisements like the following:

Health, the most estimable of temporal blessings, is, unquestionably, to mankind an object of the deepest interest, and deserving every paramount consideration. Yet, we find, that the common and most dangerous complaints of the present age, are the offspring of intemperance and sensuality. The baneful consequences of luxurious indulgences, and the effect produced by the passions of the mind on the body, invariably generate every species of NERVOUS DEBILITY. When the valetudinarian perceives himself at the brink of the grave, then his most earnest solicitude is to obtain relief, and which is only to be found in DR. VENEL'S CELEBRATED TONIC REMEDY. ... When all others have been tried in vain, this DIVINE REMEDY never can fail to give relief.

It cost 10s. 6d. per packet.

Considerable faith was formerly put in mineral springs as a means of cure:

The mineral waters of this county were formerly in high repute and some of them were much frequented. But principally owing to a change in fashion or opinion they have

28. Guy's Hospital in Southwark. 'The buildings consist of a centre and two wings. . . . The former is devoted to the reception of patients: and behind it is a small neat edifice for lunatics. . . . The wings contain the houses of the principal officers; besides which there is a theatre for medical lectures, a library well furnished with professional works, and a collection of anatomical preparations. The whole comprehends thirteen wards, and 411 beds. The out-patients also, to whom relief is extended by this institution, are very numerous.'

into the houses of the inhabitants'. But such conveniences were rare.

Lack of personal hygiene was a sure means of spreading infection, especially in the crowded dwellings of the poor. The Surrey Gaol and Bridewell indeed had four cold baths and one warm bath recently installed to guard against this hazard. Yet most large houses in Surrey lacked piped water, and fitted baths would not be a standard feature of noble houses for another fifty years. The practice was that a maid settled a large protective mat in the middle of the bedroom floor and brought ewers of hot and cold water. A hip bath was centred on the mat and in this the bather squatted. That wash lasted him for a week or so.

The privy in middle-class Surrey country houses was often located at the bottom of the garden, and it was usual to plant a large flowering shrub in front of the door. It might be a small rough-timbered building with a wooden seat and a pit underneath. It was often referred to as the 'Jericho'. Farm labourers and their families merely squatted in the corner of a field. The 'Jericho' soak-away pit was potentially a killer. It could so easily infect the parish water-supply, and it often did. A few larger mansions in important towns were beginning to be fitted with the first rudimentary water-closets.

Water was obtained by sinking a well, and often this could be the deciding factor when siting a house; otherwise it was brought in pails from the nearest street or parish pump – a favourite place for gossip. Soap was very dear and mostly out of reach of the poor. It carried a prohibitive tax in 1815 of 3*d*. per pound.

29. Near the Obelisk stood the School for the Indigent Blind (left), for teaching blind people a trade by which to earn a living. Built in 1811–12, it housed about 50 to 60 pupils, employed in making 'threads, window-sash, and clothes-line, hampers, wicker baskets of every description, bear-mats, and mats for hearths and carriages.'

now lost their reputation. The springs of this kind are those at Epsom, Cobham, Streatham; the 'Dog and Duck' in St George's Fields; Jessops Wells, Comb-hill, Kingston; Dulwich; the 'Iron Pear Tree' near Godstone; Warpesdon, Newdigate, Frensham, Witley, Meg's Well, near Dorking.

At Guildford, 'In 1775 the late Lord Grantley constructed a cold bath . . . for the convenience of the inhabitants'. Besides, 'The town is supplied with water by means of an engine, which throws it into a reservoir at the foot of Poyle-hill, whence it is conveyed by pipes

The unpleasant truth was that a room full of people was so overpoweringly smelly that only a drenching in rose water, civet, musk, or lavender from Mitcham could cover the lack of personal cleanliness.

Teeth were more often than not badly decayed; by the age of forty they were falling out through lack of even elementary care. Foetid breath was commonplace, even in Court circles. Eventually perfumed mouth pastilles became available, but a fan still remained an essential piece of equipment for crowded drawing-rooms. Tooth-whitening and tooth-cleaning preparations could be bought; these tinctures and powders contained abrasives and weak acids. A course of such patent toilet preparations hastened the day when a set of Egyptian pebble teeth had to be ordered. French dentists remained the leaders of this profession from the eighteenth to the nineteenth century. In 1800 one of them obtained a charter to manufacture baked porcelain dentures from paste supplied by the Wedgewood pottery. Toothache could, of course, be cured by the Surrey rural method of suspending a baked acorn round the neck. A more sophisticated and certain way to obtain relief was to lay roasted turnip parings behind the ear.

Many foods and drinks sold were disease-carriers or unfit for human consumption by reason of additives. At no other period have records shown merchants guilty of such flagrant adulteration of food as between 1800 and 1815. A Mr Accum, who was professor of chemistry at the Surrey Institution in Blackfriars Road, drew attention in his prolific writings to these horrid practices, and it was through his revelations that

30. The dining-hall of the Asylum for the reception of friendless and deserted girls, in Lambeth. 'The particular objects of this charity are the children of soldiers, sailors, and other indigent persons, bereft of their parents. . . . The children are to make and mend their own linen; make shirts, shifts and table-linen; to do all kinds of plain needlework, and to perform the business of the house and the kitchen. They are to be bound apprentices for seven years, at the age of fifteen, or sooner, as domestic servants to reputable families in Great Britain.'

31. The New Bethlem Hospital, in St George's Fields, was begun in 1812, as a new home for mental patients. In August 1815, 122 patients were brought here in hackney coaches from the old madhouse in Moorfields. (The building now houses the Imperial War Museum.)

efforts were made to stamp them out. Many of the adulterations had been practised for years – alum added to bread, Gloucester cheese coloured with red lead, lead in cider and wine, plaster of paris and pipe-clay in flour, chalk and flour in milk, dried blackthorn leaves added to tea. The bright colours of London confectionery were obtained by the use of highly poisonous salts of copper and lead, and chocolate was enriched with brick-dust. Some of the cheaper blends of imported butter from Holland contained as much as 33 per cent water. It was generally rancid by the time the customer bought it. It also carried a mess of the scrapings of other rejected fats, and this butter was known in the trade as 'Bosh'. Bosh is actually a Turkish word meaning worthless.

As already mentioned, the County Gaol and Bridewell (or House of Correction) stood in Southwark. 'Each felon has a cell 8 feet 3 by 6 feet 9; with iron-grated window 4 feet by 2. . . . They are furnished with an elm-plank bedstead, only 22 inches wide, a flock bed, and pillow, two blankets and a rug: the bedding is shaken and rolled up, and the cells are cleaned every morning' – recent moves for prison reform were having effect. The prisoners' bread allowance was $1\frac{1}{2}$lb. per day per person.

Twice yearly the county in general was visited by judges of the Home Circuit.

The Lent Assizes for the county of Surrey are always held at Kingston, and during that time the prisoners . . . are confined at the Stock House, and the house of correction. The Summer Assizes are once in two years at Guildford, and the prisoners then kept at the Bridewell there. Every other summer they are held at Croydon, and during the time were confined, heretofore, in stables, which are now properly converted into a large room suitable for this purpose.

Thus the 1815 summer assizes were held at Croydon on Thursday 27 July, 'but nothing of the least interest took place'. It was at the assizes that capital charges were tried, and sentences of death, transportation or whipping were freely handed out. In the early nine-teenth century a large variety of crimes were still 'punishable by the deprivation of life'. For instance, at the Old Bailey in 1815, the following crimes were punished with the death sentence: murder, rape, high treason, burglary, major theft, highway robbery, horse-stealing, sheep-stealing, house-breaking, forgery, coining and returning from transportation to an overseas colony before the term of sentence was up.

Lesser cases were tried before the J.P.s or county magistrates, at the quarter sessions held four times a year. 'When the Sessions are held at Reigate, the prisoners . . . are confined there generally for two days in the Cage, which has a strong room below, about 20 feet by 12 for the men, and above it are two rooms about 12 feet square, one for men and the other for women; they have loose straw only to sleep on.'

To cope with urban crime, Southwark had its own police office called Union Hall. On Saturday 29 July the office 'was crowded to excess, in consequence of no less than forty-one disorderly women being brought up' in custody of the constables.

The overseers of the several parishes attended, as did also a number of the respectable inhabitants, and stated that the nuisance arising from these unfortunate wretches infesting the streets was arrived at so great a height, that it was impossible for any respectable female to venture out after dark, but at the risk of having their eyes or ears offended by indecent actions and obscene language.

The magistrate committed the forty-one women to hard labour in the house of correction for fourteen days as rogues and vagrants, 'and they were immediately marched off in couples, some dressed in the first style of fashion, and others in the most wretched garb misery could assume'.

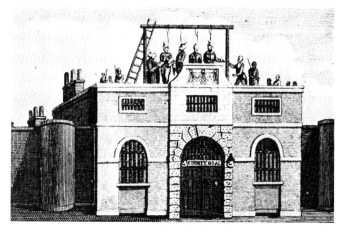

32. The County Gaol. 'This noble building does honour to the county. . . . The boundary wall encloses about three acres and a half of ground.' At the front, above the Turnkey's lodge, was a spacious lead-flat where executions were performed.

33. The main courtyard of the King's Bench Prison, in Borough Road, Southwark, 'a place of confinement for debtors'.

34. Wimbledon Villa, exotically decorated with lions and sphinxes, was just one of many elegant houses in that neighbourhood close to London.

7. Upper-class life

'Few counties in the kingdom can vie with Surrey in the number and elegance of the gentlemen's seats which it contains.' Some of these belonged to old Surrey families who had held their land for centuries, such as the Onslows of Clandon and the Evelyns of Wotton. But, as fortunes were won and lost, many landowners had arrived in the county fairly recently, attracted by its nearness to London, so that some estates had changed hands two or more times in twenty years. The neighbourhood of Richmond, Roehampton and Wimbledon was crammed with the country villas and mansions of the aristocracy and rich merchants.

'There are no very large estates in Surrey. The most extensive does not much exceed £10,000 per annum, and but few approach to that annual rent.' Comparison of this figure with the £30 annual income of a farm labourer reveals the amazing gulf between rich and poor, in an age when wealth still largely depended on ownership of land.

Political power was also tied to large-scale ownership of land. We have already seen that several influential families held Surrey boroughs in their pockets. By control of these seats in Parliament they acquired strong political power. Among the upper classes politics were looked upon as an easy road to success, and to a goal which obsessed the novelist of the period – the accummulation of a fortune. It was a wise father who got his sons into the House of Commons at an early age, and a great many did. Among the county's fourteen M.P.s there were two Onslows, two Thorntons, and two members of the Cocks family.

In fact a whole range of well-placed jobs in the Government, the Civil Service, the armed forces, and the Church were a cornucopia of golden sovereigns from which the office-holder enriched himself. Marriage to an heiress was a regular and expected way of repairing or advancing family fortunes. The hope was, of course, to marry not only into a fortune but also into an improved social position. It is this anxious unscrupulous searching for a beautiful and eligible heiress which forms the central theme of many books, plays and operas of the time.

The cheapness of hiring servants made possible the whole leisured life-style of the rich. At the burial of a Mr Moon in 1815 at Godalming, his remains were carried to the grave by six servants, 'five of whom had lived with him from 20 to 30 years, the sixth 12 years'.

Well-to-do women had little to occupy them but gossiping and spending countless hours on their appearance. At the turn of the century, fashion was changing to the Empire style, current in France, which copied the styles of ancient Greece and Rome. The hair might be worn in full curls at the front, and the back hair tied up on top with ringlets hanging down. In 1815 waists were at their highest ever, and the figure-clinging look was still in vogue. A long dress and shorter over-gown were the fashion for evening wear.

35. Evening wear of 1815, consisting of an ankle-length dress and a shorter over-gown, or *pélisse*. The hair is worn in classical curls and bound up behind.

36. Walking costume of 1815, displaying the particularly high waist-line which was fashionable that year.

A fairly recent innovation was starch to stiffen collars and cuffs.

Here are some fashions suggested for April 1815:

EVENING DRESS – White satin petticoat, ornamented at the feet with white satin trimming; a deep flounce of blond lace, gathered full into a narrow heading of corresponding trimming, and laid on in festoons above the lower border. Body white satin.

MORNING DRESS – A loose robe of cambric or worked jaconet muslin, over a petticoat of same, flounced with French trimming; long full sleeves, confined at the wrist with treble drawings, and ornamented with corresponding trimmings.

GENERAL OBSERVATIONS – Coloured satin spensers made very short in the waist, lined with white, and trimmed with swansdown, though on the decline, are not exploded. The only novelty in these spensers is the cape, which is cut up on each shoulder, and is rounded behind, but quite square in front; the sleeves, which are long and plain, are not so loose as they were worn last month.

The French bonnet is still worn; next to it is the novel Neapolitan hat, made of primrose or straw-colour pearl silk. The crown of the Neapolitan hat is narrow at the top and broad at the bottom. . . . The front is a turn-up one, broad in front and shallow behind. A short plume of feathers, either white or to correspond with the mantle, finishes this hat.

The most tasteful novelty in the carriage costume is a short French *pélisse* in white satin, lined with violet sarsenet and ornamented with violet satin.

By 1805 trousers had succeeded knee-breeches as ordinary male attire, though still not accepted as formal evening dress. In Guildford over-ripe tomatoes had been thrown at men wearing these trend-setting monstrosities. Pantaloon-trousers were introduced around 1815. Waistcoats, tailcoats and boots comprised the rest of normal dress.

The fast set had introduced the waltz; but Lord Byron thought it was a wanton exercise. The basic pursuits of most rich young men were eating, drinking, gambling and sport. Enormous meals washed down by great quantities of drink helped pass the time. Outrageous sums were spent on the furniture and fittings of the large houses where many friends could be entertained. Sir John Frederick, for example, spent £703. 10s. at Chippendale's for a few fashionable pieces for his house in Burwood Park: 'A mahogany Bason Stand with a Drawer, a Bason and Soapcups, and a mahogany Ice-Pail'.

The previous century had been a period of much building, when lavish sums were spent on houses and gardens. Surrey in 1815 could boast recent examples of work by England's best-known architects, artists and designers. The Lord Lieutenant's house at Peper-Harow was the work of Sir William Chambers (1765–8); at Hatchlands and the Oaks were rooms decorated by Robert Adam; Claremont was designed by Henry Holland and Lancelot 'Capability' Brown; the latter landscaped the park at Clandon. Dulwich College picture gallery, by Sir John Soane, was opened to the public in 1814.

More recently the classical tradition was continued by Nash at Southborough House, Surbiton (1808), by James Wyatt in the lodges at Camberley's Royal Military Academy (c.1810), and by John Perry at

37. Caricature of a middle-class party. The man on the right is in the traditional knee-breeches; another in the foreground is in trousers; and on the far left can be seen a pair of pantaloon trousers, introduced around 1815. Chinese influence is evident in the room décor.
38. Clandon Park, now open to the public, has interiors of a grandeur which adequately reflected the wealth and social position of its owners in 1815.

Godalming market hall (1814). The architecture of this period became known later as the Regency style. It was one of the most elegant styles of English architecture: the houses were the civilizing ornament of the countryside. The Regency mode called for graceful exteriors, often faced with stucco, and frequently windows were set into shallow bowed features. Inside were striped wallpaper, chintzes and beautiful iron-

39. Claremont, near Esher, built in 1772 in classical style for Clive of India. In 1816 the mansion would be purchased as a home for the Prince Regent's daughter Charlotte, after her marriage.

40. Ashtead Park, designed by Joseph Bonomi (1790) and executed by Samuel Wyatt, in a heavy classical style which has little in common with the lightness of the Regency. It is the only wholly neo-classical house in Surrey.

work. Silverware and ceramics had pleasant, light decorations. Overall there was a consistent sense of architectural proportion.

Another feature was a tendency to experiment with

42. A Chinese cabinet at Clandon Park. It typifies the experimentation with exotic styles which had been common in furniture design for some years.

41. Selsdon House, near Croydon, was designed chiefly by its owner, George Smith (a Director of the East India Company) in the neo-gothic style. It was later enlarged and converted into an hotel.

43. Thomas Hope of Deepdene, heir to a huge fortune, became absorbed with architecture at an early age, and spent eight years drawing remains of buildings in Egypt, Greece, Turkey, Syria, Sicily, Spain, and elsewhere, before settling in England in 1794.

exotic forms: Gothic, Egyptian, Chinese, rustic and Tudor. The Gothic style is found at Nonsuch House by Wyatville (1802–6), at Ewell Castle, by Henry Kitchen (1810–14), and at Selsdon House. But not only the rich benefited from the prevailing elegance of style: the streets and houses of Farnham, Guildford, Richmond and elsewhere still contain charming survivals of the period.

The interiors of houses received as much attention as the outsides: superb furniture to the designs of Chippendale, Thomas Sheraton, George Smith or Charles Tatham, gilt and mahogany beautifully proportioned with classical decorative motifs such as scrollings, tendrils, shells and palm-leaves. Gothic, Chinese and Egyptian decoration was common on armchairs, settees, sofas, tables, beds and cabinets. Slender, graceful shapes, sometimes ornamented with inlay work, decorated with urns and swags, made houses a joy to live in.

One famous furniture designer was Thomas Hope, the son of a rich merchant of Amsterdam, who came to England with his family when Holland was occupied by the French. He spent much of his large fortune on collecting ancient sculptures and vases, Dutch and Italian paintings, and other works of art. Some of these found their way to Deepdene, near Dorking, the mansion he bought in 1806.

8. Sport and leisure

Certain sports were particularly favoured by the rich, among them hunting and racing. In 1815 at least two packs of foxhounds were maintained, for the Old Surrey hunt and the Surrey Union hunt.

About two miles east of Guildford lay 'a fine circular course for horse-races; where a plate of one hundred guineas, given by William III, and three subscription plates . . . are run for in the Whitsun week.' Around this time flat-race meetings were also held at Egham, Reigate and Epsom. At Epsom it was customary to commence the sport at 11 a.m. and continue most of the day, with a break in the afternoon when people went into Epsom town for dinner. The meetings here were of little importance until the famous races for the Derby and the Oaks were established around 1780 by members of a house-party staying at the near-by house called the Oaks, belonging to the Earl of Derby, a leading sportsman of his day.

Boxing, too, was not only fashionable but was indeed a cult among the fancy. This barefist prize-fighting was strictly controlled by the very respectable Pugilistic Club. The chief contests were staged outside London, often in insignificant Surrey villages, where as many as 20,000 sportsmen might assemble. Barefist contests took place on Wimbledon Common, a large number were mounted on Epsom Downs, and many other common

44. Part of a hunt meet outside a country inn.

lands in Surrey saw a 24ft. square ring with eight stakes and two ropes set up at dawn. On 11 June 1815 the following account was published of a fight at Moulsey Hurst:

A famous day's play of Pugilism took place on Tuesday at Moseley Hurst, before a numerous assemblage of amateurs. The great match was between Scroggins, the sailor, who had distinguished himself on a different element, and Nosworthy, the baker, who was thought *terrible* from his having won with Dutch Sam, about which event so much dispute has existed. It was a sporting fight, at even betting, but Scroggins had the

45. The Oaks, Carshalton. 'Lord Derby, who was remarkable for his hospitality, had a pack of stag-hounds on this establishment, and could accommodate his guests with upwards of fifty bed-chambers.'

turn. . . . Nosworthy was knocked down at setting to in the sixth round. . . . In the eighth round Nosworthy was again knocked down. . . . He was unable to come to time after the 15th round, and his head was never out of *chancery* from the first round. The battle lasted 18 minutes. A second and most courageous battle was fought between Tom Johnson, of Paddington, and Rowe, a smith. . . . The former won in half an hour, after much good and determined fighting. Rowe received a hit at the close of the battle under the lower left rib, which sent him to sleep.

Cockfighting was another activity involving heavy gambling; Lord Derby was one who staked large sums on mains of cocks. The more important fights were highly organized affairs with strict rules of play, but there were many more casual contests. On the edge of some gathering, at an Epsom horse-race for instance, a few fanciers were usually hovering to make money from a shagbag or shakebag fight. In this kind of extempore contest the dazed bird was shaken out of his bag to do battle with another cock half-blinded by the light. Despite increasing public feeling against this cruel sport, small local fights were to continue in the depths of Surrey for many years to come.

For a long time Surrey had played a leading part in the development of English cricket, with well-established clubs all over the county. Mitcham and Epsom clubs ranked among the best in Surrey; in 1815 Epsom was strong enough to take on Hampshire, Sussex and Middlesex at different matches. A famous cricketer, Surrey born and bred, was William Lambert, perhaps unmatched as an all-round player, and said to be the 'very best batsman of his time'. He first played for Surrey in 1801, and was still playing in county matches up to 1839.

On Shrove Tuesday, 15 February 1815, a coach passenger travelling from Hampton Court to Kingston-upon-Thames was intrigued to notice at various places along the way 'all the inhabitants securing the glass of all their front windows from the ground to the roof, some by placing hurdles before them, and some by nailing laths across the frames'. It was football day! On reaching Kingston he had an opportunity to watch the whole procedure,

. . . which is, to carry a foot-ball from door to door and beg money: at about 12 o'clock the ball is turned loose, and those who can, kick it. In the town of Kingston, all the shops are purposely kept shut upon that day; there were several balls in the town, and of course several parties [groups of players]. I observed some persons of respectability following the ball: the game lasts about four hours, when the parties retire to the public houses, and spend the money they before collected in refreshments. I understand the corporation of Kingston attempted to put a stop to this practice, but the judges confirmed the right of the game, and it now legally continues, to the no small annoyance of some of the inhabitants, besides the expense and trouble they are put to in securing all their windows. . . .

Pedestrianism was a popular activity, as reported on 12 November: 'It having been stated that a man, named Eaton, a baker, had undertaken, for a considerable sum, to perform 1,100 miles in 1,100 successive hours, and Friday being the day appointed for the commencement of this extraordinary task, it attracted a motley assemblage of persons on Blackheath.' The starting-posts were fixed and the flags stationed, and he began his walk at 1.45, dressed in a blue coat, white hat and white stockings. 'He performed the first mile in 14 minutes, and then went into the Hare and Billet, where a bed and every other convenience are provided for his accommodation.' He began his second mile at 2.20, and a large crowd began to assemble. By Saturday 18 November he had completed 194 miles – 'He generally smiles when he is out a-walking'. On Saturday the 25th he was still confident, but appeared 'somewhat sorefooted'. Finally on Tuesday 26 December at

8.15 a.m. 'this individual completed his task of walking 1,100 miles in 1,100 hours, upon Blackheath', and received the cheers of a huge crowd. 'The facility with which he has executed his unexampled task, and the unimpaired vigour he has still preserved, have induced him to propose some further undertakings.'

Not far from Lambeth Palace stood Astley's Royal Amphitheatre, where superb feats of horsemanship received this review in 1815:

It is but justice to Mr Astley to say that he omits no exertion that can possibly contribute to the amusement of the town, and that he invariably produces something of a very superior

46. Despite growing public disapproval, cockfighting remained a favourite sport of the rich and idle.

47. Astley's Royal Amphitheatre was rebuilt in 1804. 'The stage is one hundred and thirty feet wide, being the largest stage in England, and extremely well adapted to the purpose for which it was built, the introduction of grand spectacles and pantomimes, wherein numerous troops of horses, are seen in what has every appearance of a real warfare, gallopping to and fro, etc. etc. . . . It is lighted by a magnificent glass chandelier suspended from the centre, and containing fifty patent lamps, and sixteen smaller chandeliers, with six wax-lights each.'

merit. To gratify holiday folks, he has this season produced a new grand equestrian spectacle entitled Ferdinand of Spain or Ancient Chivalry – which must have been produced at a considerable expense, and is supported by some of the best ballet performers. One scene in particular was loudly applauded; and was one of the best contrived and well executed exhibitions we have witnessed – the burning of the castle with falling timbers, etc. The evening's entertainment concluded with a new pantomime taken from the Arabian Nights, and called the Four Gates, or Harlequin Key; containing some excellent tricks, and a tolerable share of picturesque and beautiful scenery; the whole of the performance was very well received and continues to be received with commensurate applause.

Near the Obelisk stood the Surrey Theatre, where the programme ranged over popular opera and solo pieces. The stubborn non-cooperation of one temperamental Italian singer there in 1815 produced a flood of abuse from *Scourge* magazine, which obviously had little fear of libel action:

Let us ask how long will the English nobility suffer themselves to be degraded and insulted by a puppy of an opera singer, a fellow who very probably in his own country would be recognised to have emerged from the lowest haunts of beggarly obscurity, who had fed half his life among hogs, and for the most part of the other felt happy in collecting the crumbs in his hand that fell from a middling tradesman's table – a moving puppet without brains – a calf with a musical bleat, and no other qualification to rescue him from the ranks of an army. How long, for the miserable gratification of hearing a wretched foreigner squall his neutral-gendered notes, will the English nobility suffer themselves and their country to be degraded by such a thing, a mere animated bagpipe, a fiddle case, a musical walking-stick . . . but who will credit that where there is a Bedlam, a St Luke's and other mad houses, that the people who pay to hear this are suffered to walk about without a keeper?

At Guildford, 'a theatre was built a few years since; and here a strolling company occasionally performs'. Similarly at Richmond, 'A few years ago a theatre was erected at the north-west corner of the green. This is licensed, and opened regularly in the summer season three, and sometimes four, times in the week, and is generally supplied with performers from the London theatres.'

Diversions were plentiful and varied in those parts of the county near London. John Tribe, as a law student, walked over the bridge in the evenings to one of the coaching inns which specialized in brewing their own ale. Different inns had always sold their own brew: buttered ale warmed and flavoured with sugar, or with cinnamon and butter – wheat malt beer which went by the name of Mum and was sometimes made of oatmeal or beanmeal instead of hops. He could even find an ex-soldier innkeeper who still sold a drink called Lamb's Wool, a wholesome traditional English beverage composed of strong ale and the pulp of roasted apples with sugar and spices. He played ninepins or bowls at Epsom; with a group of boisterous friends he joined the merrymaking at Lambeth Wells or went on to Southwark Fair. At times he sampled the pleasures of Vauxhall Gardens where rich and poor mingled freely, and where he would find ample refreshment, musical entertainment, fireworks, displays of pictures and statuary.

48. Fireworks at Vauxhall. At night the pleasure gardens down to the river were lit by over a thousand lamps.

49. At Battersea was an air mill and malt distillery. 'The mill, now used for grinding malt for the distillery, was built for the grinding of linseed. . . . The outer part consists of ninety-six shutters, eight feet high, and nine inches broad, which by the pulling of a rope, open and shut in the manner of Venetian blinds. In the inside, the main shaft of the mill is the centre of a large circle formed by the sails, which consist of ninety-six double planks placed perpendicularly, and of the same height as the planks that form the shutters. The wind rushing through the openings of these shutters, acts with great power upon the sails, and when it blows fresh, turns the mill with prodigious rapidity. . . . In this mill are six pairs of stones.'

9. Industry

In 1815 stone quarries were operated near Godstone, Gatton, Merstham, Reigate and Blechingley. 'Large quarries of lime-stone near Dorking afford lime equal in purity and strength to any in the kingdom. It is particularly serviceable for works under water.' It was used in constructing some of the London docks. Limestone was also dug at Guildford, Sutton and Carshalton. The sand about Tandridge, Dorking and Reigate was in heavy demand for making hour-glasses.

That useful material, fuller's earth, is found in great quantities about Nutfield, Reigate and Blechingley to the south of the downs; and some, but of inferior quality, north of them near Sutton and Croydon. There are two kinds, the blue and the yellow, which are used for different purposes; the latter being chiefly employed in fulling the fine cloths of Wiltshire and Gloucestershire, and the former sent into Yorkshire for the coarser manufactures.

Fuller's earth, a peculiar species of clay, had always been the most important mineral product of the county. Found in beds varying in depth from four to fourteen feet, it was very easy to mine. Its qualities of absorbing all oil and grease from woollen cloth had been known for hundreds of years – it was, in fact, so valuable in the preparation of English cloth that its export had once been forbidden. Around 1815 four pits were operating at Nutfield and Reigate; no more than a dozen men were employed but the output was up to 3,000 tons yearly. Considerable quantities were transported on the horse-drawn iron railway from Merstham to Croydon, and from there to London, either along the Croydon canal or by the iron railway to Wandsworth, where it could be shipped on the Thames. Fuller's earth required no other preparation to fit it for market than the removal of every trace of rust. It was thoroughly dried by the fullers and ground in a mill to a fine powder before it could be applied to cloth.

Gunpowder-making was also long-established in the county. Gunpowder-mills could be seen on the banks of the Wey, four mills derived power from the Tilling-bourne (including the famous Chilworth mills), and about a dozen stood beside the Hogsmill at Ewell and neighbourhood.

Despite the invention of the steam-engine, very many industries used water power. The river Wandle, ten miles long, was thought to be the hardest-worked river of its size in the world. It powered up to 40 different industrial concerns, including calico-printing works, flour-mills, snuff-mills, bleaching grounds, oil-mills and dyeing works.

Calico-printing works were well established at Mitcham, Merton, Wimbledon and Wandsworth. The premises of the old palace of Croydon were now used for a 'calico-printing manufactory and bleaching-ground', and there was also a bleaching-ground at Carshalton.

The manufacture of woollen cloth had been the staple industry of Guildford, Godalming and region –

50. Near Waterloo Bridge stood the manufactory for patent shot established around 1789 by Messrs Watts. 'The principle of making this shot is to let it fall from a great height, that it may cool and harden in its passage through the air, to such a degree as not to lose its spherical shape by the pressure of the water in which it is received below. The height of the tower at this manufactory is 140 feet, and the shot falls 123 feet.'

At Albury on the Tillingbourne a corn-mill was converted into a paper-mill around 1815. There were also paper-mills at Eashing and Carshalton. Holstein House in Weybridge had been taken over by a Mr Hamilton as a printing office 'in which about sixty men are employed'.

Of Cobham it was said: 'The principal manufactory in this town is Mr Raby's iron and copper works.' There were two iron foundries in Lambeth, and copper mills at Wimbledon and Merton.

Though the small towns away from London had their own thriving industries, most of the county's trades were strung along the south bank of the Thames, opposite London. Of Wandsworth it could be said:

The art of dying cloth has been practised at this place for more than a century. There are likewise several considerable manufactories, one for bolting cloth; iron mills; the calico printing manufactories; manufactory for printing kersey-meres; for whitening and pressing stuffs; linseed oil and white-lead mills; oil mill; vinegar works; and distilleries.

At the iron mills were cast 'shot, shell, cannon, and other implements of war'. Another shot manufactory was that of Messrs Watts in Lambeth.

Bermondsey is a place of very great trade. The tanners . . . are very numerous, and carry on that business to a greater extent than is known in any other part of the kingdom. From a natural connection between the several trades, there are also many woolstaplers, fellmongers, curriers, and leather-dressers, and some parchment-makers. [There were also some pin and needle makers.]

At this period, too, the hat-making trade flourished

good pasture on the Downs for sheep; plenty of water and fuller's earth. But by 1815 the trade had very sadly dwindled. Godalming was still producing some kerseys and other cloths, but 'the business principally carried on at present is the manufacture of silk and worsted for stockings, gloves, etc. . . . In the vicinity of the place are three paper mills.'

51. The old Tabard Inn, the most famous in Southwark, was mentioned in Chaucer's *Canterbury Tales*. From its courtyard the company of pilgrims set out together.

in Bermondsey, which was called 'the hatters' paradise', and in Southwark. Hats were traditionally made in Wandsworth also. Fleeing from religious oppression more than a century before, a colony of French protestants had settled there, having a secret process for preparing furs and skins for use in making headgear. At the height of their prosperity they received orders for hats from foreign nobility, but by 1815 this Wandsworth trade was in considerable decline.

Lambeth was well-known for its delft pottery. After several years' apprenticeship at a stoneware works in Fulham, John Doulton, along with John Watts, set up a small pottery in Vauxhall Walk. This was the forerunner of Messrs Doulton & Co. of Lambeth, whose products became world-famous. In Lambeth there were half-a-dozen potteries turning out bottles for blacking, ginger-beer, porter, cider, spruce beer, ink, oil and pickles. The oldest pottery in England was claimed to be the Vauxhall Pottery of Messrs Wagstaffe & Co., who also ran a pottery in Mortlake. In Mortlake there was another small manufactory, Kishere's, whose main articles were the so-called Toby Philpot jugs of brown stoneware ornamented with hunting scenes. The pottery trade was fairly common in Surrey: a new pottery had recently opened in Nonsuch Park at Ewell. Other products of Lambeth's industries included soap, floor-cloth, whiting, starch, salt petre, varnish, pumps, engines, coaches and harness.

Routes to London from the Continent and southern England converged on London Bridge. To meet the needs of travellers a great number of inns were opened, and in Southwark stood the chief breweries of Surrey.

Best known was the Anchor brewery, belonging to Barclay, Perkins & Co. At this period the firm concentrated on brewing porter – a dark-brown bitterish beer originally made for porters and labourers – and was recently reported as brewing 270,000 barrels in a year. The brewery extended over nearly six acres, and contained stabling sufficient for 126 horses. It employed about 200 people and 60 waggons.

A vast quantity of drink was put out from the Surrey breweries in 1815. Kingston, Wandsworth, Putney, Mortlake, among many other towns and villages throughout the county, had thriving breweries. It was hard to throw a pewter pot without hitting a brewing-master. A most effective election promise was made in 1815 by Mr Barclay, the prospective candidate for Southwark: 'My electors shall have porter at threepence a pint.' He was elected.

10. Epilogue

Looking back on Surrey in 1815, one notes the puzzling fact that while the Napoleonic wars continued, many poor men found themselves prosperous for the first time in their life. Immediately Wellington gained his remarkable victory they reverted to poverty.

In 1815 England was blessed with a good harvest. To those unacquainted with the tortuous channels of economics, it is hard to understand how this factor worsened the plight of the working man. Surely plentiful wheat meant cheap bread? And wasn't bread his staple diet? But mixed in with the dough was political yeast – a souring agent at any time.

At the same time the growth of population was phenomenal. One hundred years earlier, the vast majority of people seldom moved from the place where they had been born and bred. By 1815 there had been a movement to fertile urban counties like Surrey and, of course, to London and other industrial centres. The population map had by then adjusted to the general pattern of the twentieth century, although much thinner on the ground. So it can be seen that the Industrial Revolution not only changed people's work habits and social conditions, but impelled them to move to different areas in an attempt to better their lives.

The decade around 1815 not only produced exceptional harvests of grain, it brought out an unbelievable fruiting of literary genius – William and Mary Wordsworth, Coleridge, Byron, Blake, Scott, Lamb, Shelley, Hazlitt, Southey, Moore, De Quincey, Leigh Hunt, Crabbe, Jane Austen, and a host of others. Besides these there were many great painters, musicians, architects, dramatists, actors and inventors working in the fine arts.

At no period was Surrey so beautiful, despite terrible events and the periods of hunger and unemployment which its farm labourers faced. The hedges were full of Shepherd's Rose, Honeysuckle, and all manner of wild flowers. There were meadows green with lush grass; fruit trees heavy with red, ripe fruit; the great corn harvest giving the lie to political price-juggling; huge stands of timber stood ready for British men o'war.

Looking over the Surrey countryside William Cobbett asked, 'What that men invented under the name of pleasure grounds can equal these fields?'

What indeed!

Further Reading

Allen, Thomas. *History of the counties of Surrey and Sussex.* 2 vols. 1829–30.

Besant, Sir Walter. *South London.* 1899.

Brayley, E.W. *The beauties of England and Wales.* Vol. XIV. 1813.

Brayley, E.W. *A topographical history of Surrey.* 5 vols. 1841–48, 1850.

Clinch, G., and Kershaw, S.W. (ed.). *Bygone Surrey.* 1895. Reprinted 1970.

Cobbett, William. *Rural rides in Surrey, Kent, Sussex, Hampshire, etc.* 1830.

Cooke, G.A., *The modern British traveller.* Vol. XVII. 1817.

Cromwell, T.K. *Excursion through England and Wales, Scotland and Ireland.* 1820.

Davis, John. *Historical records of the Second Royal Surrey Regiment of Militia.* 1877.

Doncaster, I.K. *Social conditions of England 1760–1830.* 1964.

Greenwood, C. and J. *Surrey described.* 1823.

Hillier, J.R. *Old Surrey water mills.* 1951.

Lysons, D. *The environs of London.* 2nd Edition. 1811.

Manning, Owen, and Bray, William. *History and antiquities of the county of Surrey.* 3 vols. 1804–14.

Marshall, William. *The rural economy of the Southern Counties.* 1799.

Parker, Eric. *Surrey.* 1947.

Pevsner, N. *Surrey* (Buildings of England series), 1971.

Stevenson, William. *General view of the agriculture of the county of Surrey.* 1813.

Places to visit

(All opening times should be checked.)

Clandon Park, near Guildford. An eighteenth-century classical mansion belonging to the National Trust. Open to the public on certain days between April and October.

Claremont, Esher. Built in 1772 by 'Capability' Brown. Open on certain days between February and November.

Cuming Museum, Walworth Road, Southwark, London SE17. Exhibits of the history of Southwark and district.

Dulwich College Picture Gallery, College Road, London SE21. Housed in a building of 1814. Weekdays (except Mondays) and Sundays (Summer only).

Hatchlands, East Clandon. Has interiors by Robert Adam. Open on Wednesdays and Saturdays between April and September.

Kew Gardens, Kew. Royal Botanic Gardens. Open all year except Christmas Day.

Kew Palace, Kew (Dutch House). Contains souvenirs of George III. Open April to September.

Polesden Lacey, near Dorking. An original Regency villa altered in the Edwardian period. Open March to December, on certain days.